# Cambridge Elements

### Elements in New Religious Movements
Series Editor
**Rebecca Moore**
*San Diego State University*
Founding Editor
†James R. Lewis
*Wuhan University*

# ABUSE IN NEW RELIGIOUS MOVEMENTS

Sarah Harvey
*Inform, King's College London*

Shaftesbury Road, Cambridge CB2 8EA, United Kingdom

One Liberty Plaza, 20th Floor, New York, NY 10006, USA

477 Williamstown Road, Port Melbourne, VIC 3207, Australia

314–321, 3rd Floor, Plot 3, Splendor Forum, Jasola District Centre, New Delhi – 110025, India

103 Penang Road, #05–06/07, Visioncrest Commercial, Singapore 238467

Cambridge University Press is part of Cambridge University Press & Assessment, a department of the University of Cambridge.

We share the University's mission to contribute to society through the pursuit of education, learning and research at the highest international levels of excellence.

www.cambridge.org
Information on this title: www.cambridge.org/9781009660839

DOI: 10.1017/9781009660853

© Sarah Harvey 2025

This publication is in copyright. Subject to statutory exception and to the provisions of relevant collective licensing agreements, with the exception of the Creative Commons version the link for which is provided below, no reproduction of any part may take place without the written permission of Cambridge University Press & Assessment.

An online version of this work is published at doi.org/10.1017/9781009660853 under a Creative Commons Open Access license CC-BY-NC 4.0 which permits re-use, distribution and reproduction in any medium for non-commercial purposes providing appropriate credit to the original work is given and any changes made are indicated. To view a copy of this license visit https://creativecommons.org/licenses/by-nc/4.0

When citing this work, please include a reference to the DOI 10.1017/9781009660853

First published 2025

*A catalogue record for this publication is available from the British Library*

ISBN 978-1-009-66083-9 Hardback
ISBN 978-1-009-66086-0 Paperback
ISSN 2635-232X (online)
ISSN 2635-2311 (print)

Cambridge University Press & Assessment has no responsibility for the persistence or accuracy of URLs for external or third-party internet websites referred to in this publication and does not guarantee that any content on such websites is, or will remain, accurate or appropriate.

For EU product safety concerns, contact us at Calle de José Abascal, 56, 1°, 28003 Madrid, Spain, or email eugpsr@cambridge.org

# Abuse in New Religious Movements

Elements in New Religious Movements

DOI: 10.1017/9781009660853
First published online: November 2025

---

Sarah Harvey
*Inform, King's College London*
**Author for correspondence:** Sarah Harvey, sarah.harvey@kcl.ac.uk

**Abstract:** This Element analyses issues of abuse in new religious movements (NRMs). It argues that abuse in NRMs is not unique but that certain factors can be intensified in NRM contexts – propensities for separation from wider society, teachings on unique legitimacy and exclusivity and charismatic authority. First, a historical overview addresses how abuse in NRMs has been approached and understood, linking this to the development of NRM and cultic studies and their preferred terminology. Second, a theoretical framework allows consideration of the ways in which the interlinked structural and cultural factors of religious movements can contribute to the perpetration, legitimisation or concealment of abuse. Finally, the Element presents an applied case study analysing the interplay of these factors in the Jesus Fellowship Church, a UK-based NRM which closed in 2019, partly in recognition of abuses that had occurred. This title is also available as Open Access on Cambridge Core.

**Keywords:** abuse, New Religious Movements, cults, Jesus Fellowship Church, gender and sexuality

© Sarah Harvey 2025

ISBNs: 9781009660839 (HB), 9781009660860 (PB), 9781009660853 (OC)
ISSNs: 2635-232X (online), 2635-2311 (print)

# Contents

1 Introduction  1

2 A Theoretical Model of Abuse: Structural and Cultural Factors  12

3 'A Holy Segregation Between the Sexes': The Jesus Fellowship Church  36

4 Conclusion  58

References  62

# 1 Introduction

This Element addresses abuse in new religious movements (NRMs). Abuse in both old and new religious movements, historical cases and new, are increasingly coming to public notice and being examined in policy and legal contexts, in popular culture and in various academic disciplines. While this is a relatively recent area of analysis in the discipline of religious studies and mainstream sociology of religion – arguably emerging from the widespread exposé of child sexual abuse in the Catholic Church in the early 2000s – it has long been a focus in the study of new religious movements. This is a field comprising two historically polarised disciplines: NRM or new religions studies and cultic studies. The issue of abuse is inherently connected with the development of these disciplines and with the terms that they use: that is, minority or new religious movement *versus* cult. Abuse is considered a defining feature of cults, whereas NRM studies developed partly as a reaction against this coupling. This is not to say that NRM scholars have not highlighted issues of abuse, as the literature drawn on throughout this Element shows. However, it has not necessarily been their focus. In this Introduction, I set out what is meant by the terms new religious movement, minority religion, cult and abuse. This is best done through a brief history of the development of NRM and cultic studies.[1] I analyse definitions used within these fields and how scholars have addressed the issue of abuse.

In Section 2 of this Element, I suggest a theoretical model of structural and cultural factors which could be potential contributing factors to abuse and/or barriers to reporting and addressing abuse. These factors are drawn from both the theoretical literature outlined in the Introduction, and from analysis of examples of NRMs from a scholarly database of religious movements. I briefly outline six structural and six cultural factors before analysing in more depth four groupings of factors. In Section 3, I use the theoretical model to analyse the abuses that occurred in a British-based and now defunct NRM, the Jesus Fellowship Church (JFC).

The research on which this Element draws was undertaken as part of an Arts and Humanities Research Council funded project, Abuse in Religious Contexts. This project, which ran from March 2022 to June 2024, led by Gordon Lynch, comprised seven different pieces of work.[2] My own piece of work was an analysis of the 200 or so NRMs that had been marked with the theme of abuse on the Inform database of religious movements. This initial mapping exercise recorded the allegations of abuse; the sources of information (noting,

---

[1] See Ashcraft (2018) for a more detailed analysis of the history of these fields.
[2] See https://blogs.ed.ac.uk/airc/.

unfortunately, a preponderance of media sources); whether there had been legal cases; structural (organisational) and cultural (beliefs and practices) factors which were mentioned in relation to abuse; and outcomes, such as internal or external investigations and apologies by leadership. I then looked in greater depth at the approximately fifty movements about which Inform held more in-depth information, including enquiries to Inform and internal or external investigation reports. Some of the fifty movements are discussed briefly throughout this Element with one selected as the applied case study based on the wealth of information, including its own reports and responses to charges.

Inform (Information Network on Religious Movements) is an educational charity founded by sociologist of religion Eileen Barker in 1988 in order to provide information about minority religions and sects which is as accurate, up-to-date and as evidence-based as possible. I have been a researcher at Inform since 2001, and my twenty years of experience with Inform, an organisation established firmly on the NRM studies side of the cult wars, places me within the NRM studies field. The factors discussed in this Element arise out of my theoretical grounding in NRM studies and my experience as a researcher at Inform. However, they were refined both by analysis of specific movements and by discussions in project meetings with other members of the Abuse in Religious Contexts team.

## 1.1 A Brief History of NRM and Cultic Studies

The categorisation of religion into different types has its origins in the foundations of the discipline of sociology. In the early twentieth century, sociologists created typologies of forms of religion with attention to a religion's relationship with its social environment. The crux of these typologies is the distinction between church and sect, created by Weber (1922) and Troeltsch (1931), church being open to all and in alignment with the social order, sect being in tension with society, setting itself apart and accepting only religious adepts. This model was refined over time. Niebuhr (1929) added the concept of denomination to indicate the transformation and accommodation of a sect after the first generation of converts; Becker (1932) created a four-fold typology consisting of denomination and ecclesia, sect and cult; and Yinger (1946) further developed the cult category to indicate groups which break from the dominant norms and traditions of society, unlike sects which are schisms from a church. Cult and sect were defined by their state of tension with wider society, unlike church and denomination, which were in alignment with society. Although these were intended as technical, sociological terms with wide applicability, from the outset their origins in and applicability to a Christian, Western social context was clear. The term 'cult', however, did not originate within sociology.

The Latin *cultus* is used to refer to worship, veneration or adoration of a particular figure, saint or deity, for example, the cult of the Virgin Mary. In some academic disciplines, including archaeology and ancient history, this usage is retained. The use of cult as a label for a problematic religion has been linked with mid-nineteenth-century Protestant movements' theological critiques of new Christian sects such as the Church of Jesus Christ of Latter-day Saints – popularly known as Mormons – and Jehovah's Witnesses, as well as new spiritual movements such as Theosophy and Spiritualism (Ashcraft 2018; Zeller 2023; Chryssides 2024). From a normative, Protestant perspective, these movements were considered dangerous heresies. Critiques remained largely theological until the mid-twentieth century. Wider usage of the term 'cult' to indicate a controversial or bad religion, or indeed not a real religion, entered public discourse with a concern around Western youth's turn to new and alternative spiritual movements during the counterculture of the 1960s. For numerous intersecting reasons, including the rise of youth culture, a breaking of adherence to established rules and traditions – including Church membership – and the relaxing of immigration regulations, Western youth were exposed to new religious movements and had the financial, social and temporal capital to commit to them for the first time. This was framed as dangerous by some, including the young people's families, the established churches and media. Academics, on the other hand, largely approached this as an interesting rise in new forms of religiosity and meaning-making.

As noted by numerous authors (Beckford 1985; Barker 2014, 2017; Gallagher 2017; Ashcraft 2018; Chryssides 2024), this situation developed into the cult wars of the 1980s and 1990s in which the field became polarised between cultic studies scholars, often associated with psychology, counselling and mental health professionals, and NRM studies scholars, often associated with sociology, history, and religious studies, but also including scholars from the fields of law, psychology and psychiatry. Cultic studies scholars contributed to a wider anticult or cult awareness movement (Barker 2002a; Giambalvo et al. 2013) which sought to warn the public about the dangers of cults and, at times, to campaign for legislation to restrict their activities or ban them outright. NRM studies scholars saw the anticult practices of kidnapping members to 'deprogram' them as 'human rights violations' (Barker 2014: 251), and converts' agency and choice as a religious freedom issue was a guiding principle.

Points of difference between the two fields hinged to some extent on the definition of cult, its inherent link with concepts of harm, abuse and danger, and the issue of brainwashing. Cultic studies scholars prioritised ex-members' testimonies while NRM scholars were generally sceptical of the extent of their value, arguing that the ex-members who spoke out were those who had negative experiences and were critical of their former movements (Bromley 1998). These testimonies were described as atrocity stories by some (e.g. Wilson 1990). A focus on ex-members who went public with their stories missed the perspective of those who left for more prosaic reasons it was argued (Chryssides and Gregg 2019). NRM scholars also noted the high attrition rates of the movements, indicating that people clearly could join and leave of their own accord (Barker 1984; Beckford 1985). Some NRM scholars, informed by sociological research methods, sought to include all perspectives on a religious movement in the belief that an objective picture could then be portrayed. Barker, writing about the methodology of Inform, has written 'not only should the methodological techniques be as varied as possible, but that as wide a range as possible of the different actors affecting the situation should be studied in their own right and taken together' (2011: 25). In this, she rejects the view that one should commit themselves to research either with leavers or with members. As a student of Barker and an employee of Inform, I too am committed to this principle of triangulation. However, it should be noted that this Element is part of a survivor-centred project; inevitably then, survivor voices and accounts of abuse are prioritised within this Element. It also stands in an emerging tradition among a fresh generation of NRM scholars who missed the cult wars of the 1970s and 1980s who are reconsidering ideas on issues of objectivity, subjectivity, reflexivity and former member accounts (Thomas and Graham-Hyde 2024). Scholars such as Thomas and Graham-Hyde have acknowledged, for instance, an historical overreliance on 'insider experience' and a neglect of 'the valuable testimonies of ex-members' in NRM studies (2024: 9). Their work, and this Element, is an attempt at an intervention and rebalancing from within the field.

There is no single agreed-upon definition of cult, but prominent cultic studies authors (Hassan 1988; Langone 1994, 2015; Dubrow-Marshall 2024) and organisations[3] convey similar ideas with the term. These largely draw upon Lifton's (1961) eight principles of 'thought reform' or brainwashing developed in the context of American prisoners of war held in Korea in the 1950s. These eight principles – milieu control, mystical manipulation, demand for purity, confession, sacred science, loading the language, doctrine over person and dispensing of existence – remain important factors in analysing the dynamics of some religious and social movements. They bear similarity to some of the

---

[3] The most important of which is now the American-based International Cultic Studies Association (ICSA) – https://internationalculticstudies.org/ – founded as the American Family Foundation in 1979.

factors of abuse I discuss in this Element. However, they are not true of all NRMs, and neither is it true that converts to an NRM are brainwashed (Barker 1984).[4] More recent definitions of the term cult contain similar checklists such as Hassan's (1988) 'BITE Model of Authoritarian Control' and Langone's (2015) 'Characteristics Associated with Cultic Groups'. Following Lifton, these models describe ways in which individuals are controlled to the detriment of their own health and wellbeing and for the gratification of a charismatic leader. They include such factors as unquestioning commitment to the leader, mind-altering practices, such as meditation and chanting, a preoccupation with recruitment and/or making money, converts cutting ties with family and friends and dedicating all of their time to the movement.

These practices have led to a more recent conceptualisation of high-demand or high-control movements.[5] These models are concerned with issues of manipulation, undue influence, control and deception, and the propensity for abuse and harm that can follow. Some of these factors are certainly true of some NRMs. There are overlaps with some of the factors which can enable abuse that I will discuss. The significant difference is that NRM scholars approach these factors as behaviours present in some groups some of the time, including in mainstream or established religions, rather than as inherently defining characteristics. Of course, there have also been developments in cultic studies over time and some authors associated with ICSA have also written about cultic properties being on a continuum and as interactionist. Rosedale and Langone (2015) note that because of this definitional ambiguity, ICSA does not produce a list of cults but rather directs 'inquirers' attention to potentially harmful practices, rather than to a label'. This is no different from the practice at Inform. In practical, day-to-day work, rather than in theoretical literature, there is arguably greater convergence between some areas of NRM and cultic studies. Barker has been pivotal in this practical convergence as ICSA's current philosophy of dialogue has been influenced by her approach (ICSA 2013).

NRM scholars argue that the term 'cult' is too pejorative to be of scholarly use, being little more than a label to indicate deviance and illegitimacy (Barker 2004; Wessinger 2008; Laycock 2022; Zeller 2023; Thomas and Graham-Hyde 2024). They argue that its use as a definitional tool is bound up with a priori assumptions about religious movements. It serves to de-humanise members,

---

[4] For further analysis of the brainwashing debate see Barker (1984), Anthony (1990), Zablocki and Robbins (2001), Reichert, Richardson and Thomas (2015), Ashcraft (2018), Moore (2018) and Introvigne (2022a). It is important to note that in the 1987 Molko legal case, the American Psychological Association stated that the theory of brainwashing was not accepted in the scientific community, a ruling that was reinforced in the 1990 Fishman legal case and which has remained into the present (Introvigne 2022a).

[5] See Laycock (2024) for a more in-depth discussion of these terms.

eradicating their agency in its linkage with brainwashing narratives and sometimes legitimising excessive action against movements by governments and law enforcement, such as the siege of the Branch Davidian compound at Waco in 1993, or laws in China criminalising *xie jiao* – heterodox teachings. These scholars argue, following Barker, that brainwashing is 'little more than a metaphor that expresses the speaker's distaste for the end result of a process of conversion, without actually explaining the process itself' (Barker 2009: 11). In contrast, cultic studies scholars argue that the term 'cult' is valuable *because* of its negative connotations: it can act as a label to signify certain controversial practices, for example, manipulation techniques, coercive relationships, abuse and violence. It should not then be restricted to religious movements but can be applied to any organisation which displays such tendencies, including street gangs, organised crime groups and terrorist organisations (Dubrow-Marshall 2024). In fact, Dubrow-Marshall (2024) distinguishes between cult and NRM as two separate entities: NRMs are not more likely to be cults than other non-religious organisations. He suggests that this inaccurate conflation has led to the circular academic arguments of the cult wars.

Nevertheless, the term 'new religious movement' was popularised by scholars of religion who sought a less value-laden label to describe groups that became visible in the 1960s and 1970s. 'New' initially had a temporal dimension, with scholars citing the mid-1940s (Wallis 1984), 1950s (Barker 1989) or 1960s (Beckford 1985) as the significant start date for marking the current rise of NRMs. This was a practical device, with recognition that many movements had much older origins, and over time scholars have refined their definitions. Melton has argued that NRMs have no shared characteristics in terms of 'beliefs, practices, or attributes' and that the 'new' should therefore refer to tension with society (2004: 73). NRMs are assigned a fringe status by dominant forces in society, both because members disagree with the beliefs, norms and values of the society and because they engage in activities deemed unacceptable, 'such as violence, illegal behavior, high pressure proselytism, unconventional sexual contacts, or minority medical practices' (Melton 2004: 73). In this they differ from sects, which 'dissent but within acceptable limits' (2004: 78) thus retaining the possibility of evolving into churches. Barker, on the other hand, has argued that new religions do share characteristics based on their newness, and it is 'as a consequence of their newness' that they are relegated to the fringes of society (2004: 88). She focuses on newness not as a temporal quality but in relation to membership. She defines new religions as consisting 'predominantly of first-generation members' (converts) and that particular characteristics follow from this (2004: 94). These characteristics include the enthusiasm with which members hold their beliefs and the NRM's desire to keep its members separate from the world to protect these beliefs; a dichotomous worldview, in which people are divided into members and non-members, us and them; the frequency of charismatic leadership in NRMs; and the movement's propensity to change more rapidly and radically than older religions. Movements become less new and, often, less in tension with society as second and subsequent generations arrive (Barker 2014). Using this definition raises some important questions about the possible characteristics of those religions that have a significant number of converts in addition to members born into the movements, such as the Church of Jesus Christ of Latter-day Saints and Jehovah's Witnesses. More recently, Singler and Barker (2022) have defined NRMs as having three characteristics: a first generation of converts, a leader with charismatic authority and beliefs and practices alternative to the mainstream.

The classic NRMs of the 1960s and 1970s, such as the Unification Church, the Church of Scientology and the International Society for Krishna Consciousness (ISKCON), now have subsequent generations and have changed significantly, due in part to the deaths of their charismatic founders, somewhat refuting their categorisation as NRMs with a first generation of converts and charismatic leaders. However, an alternative term to NRM has not been agreed upon. Minority religion is one possible term which has both pros and cons. Minority is a contextual term, always existing in relation to the majority, and hence differs according to geographical location and time period. It is a political term, indicating the process through which a group of people are 'othered' in a process of 'minoritization' (Stausberg et al. 2023). It is the term favoured by Inform, whose remit also encompasses new movements within mainstream traditions and intra-faith relationships (Newcombe and Harvey 2024). Graham-Hyde (2023) found that members of religious movements preferred the term to NRM but that it was not well-recognised within public discourse. Thomas and Graham-Hyde (2024) nevertheless advocate academic usage of the term 'minority religion' to replace both NRM and cult. Ashcraft, however, argues that other terms, including minority religion, have not 'achieved widespread usage like NRM has' (2018: 4). In this Element, I largely stick with the term 'NRM' as this best characterises the case study on which I draw to illustrate factors which can lead to a propensity for abuse. I turn now to the issue of how NRM scholars have addressed issues of violence and abuse.

## Approaches to Abuse and Violence in NRM Studies

If cultic studies scholars approach cults from an assumption of harm, it could be argued that NRM studies scholars approach NRMs from an assumption that they are not necessarily problematic, or at least are innocent until proven guilty. Generally, NRM scholars approach the study of these new movements no differently than that of mainstream religions – describing their beliefs, practices, history, leadership, membership composition and their interactions with wider society. Sometimes they focus on controversial issues, including abuse and violence. In a presentation at the 2002 ICSA conference, Barker noted that

> Sociologists who study new religions/cults/sects are trying to find out what these movements are like – what they believe, what they do, how they organise themselves, how they interact with the rest of society, and so on. They do not orient their research toward looking specifically at the harmful or the non-harmful aspects of the movements, but the harmful and non-harmful aspects will form part of their overall description, which they try to make as reliable and objective as possible. (2002b: n.p.)

She goes on to state that some of the characteristics of new religious movements can 'predispose' them 'toward situations in which harm might ensue'. Ethnographies and articles which have analysed children raised within NRMs in particular have not shied away from addressing the issue of harm (Rochford and Heinlein 1998; van Eck Duymaer van Twist 2015; Palmer 2016; Frisk et al. 2018; Barker 2022; Nilsson 2024).

However, the conceptualisation of harm in NRM studies has tended to be on 'deadly' or 'lethal' violence – 'either suicide or homicide' (Ashcraft 2018: 177). Scholars have tended to focus on the 'big six' internationally renowned cases of Jonestown, the Branch Davidians, the Order of the Solar Temple, Aum Shinrikyo, Heaven's Gate and the Movement for the Restoration of the Ten Commandments of God.[6] Important anthologies which analyse these cases include Wessinger (2000), Bromley and Melton (2002) and Lewis (2011, 2014). These NRM studies scholars have developed interactionist models of violence to explore the internal and external factors which can contribute to situations of violence. Internal factors include some of the characteristics of NRMs described by Barker (2004), such as charismatic leadership, a dualistic worldview, millennial beliefs and a degree of social isolation. This suggests that there is something in the structure of NRMs which lends itself to situations of violence. However, internal factors alone are not a sufficient explanation as the vast majority of NRMs do not turn to violence. The interactionist model suggests that violence may occur as a reaction to external factors, which can include the movement's relationship with wider society and/or an anticult or

---

[6] It now seems likely that what has become known as the 'Shakahola forest incident' or the 'Kenya starvation cult' will be added to this list. In spring 2023 it emerged that over 400 members of the Good News International Church had starved themselves to death, apparently on the direction of leader Paul Nthenge Mackenzie. See e.g. www.bbc.co.uk/news/world-africa-65412822.

media campaign against it. These can create a 'deviance amplification spiral' (Wilkins 1967; Cohen 1972) in which each side sees the other side's actions as justifying an ever-increasing stronger reaction. Building on this, Bromley (2002, 2011) has outlined a four-stage process through which the interaction of internal and external factors can result in violence: latent tension, nascent conflict, intensified conflict and dramatic denouement. A dramatic denouement, he suggests, occurs when either the religious movement or their opponents or both simultaneously, 'embark on a project of violent final reckoning that is intended to reestablish appropriate moral order' (2011: 15). This processual model highlights how, even in what are now considered stereotypical cases such as Jonestown and the Branch Davidians, violent endings were not inevitable.

These models have done a great deal in extending understandings of NRMs and violence. However, it could be argued that in the stress on lethal violence, NRM studies scholars have neglected other forms of violence. Of course, this is a generalisation to some extent and the authors referenced above do note other forms of violence, such as child abuse and sexual violence. Feminist analyses of sexual violence within NRMs exist but have not made a huge mark in the field. Jacobs (1989, 1991) was one of the first NRM scholars to take a critical feminist perspective, analysing sexual violence against women as part of an experience of failed expectations of male leaders which resulted in women leaving NRMs. Jacobs highlights that some women in NRMs experienced gender-based violence in ways which men did not, and that most NRMs replicate patriarchal authority structures, even when they claim not to. These arguments were taken up by a handful of scholars including Palmer (1994), Neitz and Goldman (1995), Puttick (1997) and Goldman (1999). Some of these scholars, including Palmer and Goldman, focused not on abuses experienced but on the reasons why women joined new religions with alternative gender roles and sexual practices, and on the significance of sex and gender in salvation (see also Section 2 below). These women scholars remain important voices in NRM studies but they are few in number. More recently, Jacobs (2007) has further reflected on the lack of attention on sexual violence in NRM studies. She suggests that NRM studies, influenced by the sociology of religion, has in the main presented a positive and normalising view of NRMs by focusing on issues of religious freedom and meaning-making. Sexual violence did not fit into this picture – but it also did not fit the concept of violence which stressed murder and mass suicide. This narrow understanding of violence neglects other forms of violence in NRMs. Gendered abuse is to be found particularly in NRMs with 'a charismatic social structure that is patriarchal in nature' (Jacobs 2007: 234). She suggests that if broader theoretical perspectives and definitions of violence are employed, it is possible to see abuse in NRMs not as a unique phenomenon but as part of 'the larger context of gendered power relations in a patriarchal culture' (2007: 239). It is then possible to look for patterns of abuse across all forms of religious movements, old and new.

## Definitions of Abuse

Referencing Jacobs's work, Ashcraft suggests that 'The field of NRM studies needs a wider definition of violence' (2018: 178). He notes that, on the whole, it is cultic studies scholars who have analysed violence and that NRM studies scholars could benefit from more engagement with their publications. In this Element, I draw on Barker's list of characteristics of NRMs, analyses of NRMs and violence, feminist critiques of NRMs and on sources from beyond NRM studies to outline structural and cultural factors which could enable abuse in religious movements. The term 'abuse', rather than violence, incorporates a wider perspective than has typically been indicated by NRM studies of violence. Drawing upon the work of the Abuse in Religious Contexts project, this Element defines abuse as 'a person's experience of serious harm or exploitation caused by someone who has some form of religious power or control in relation to them'. The experience of harm 'can be physical, sexual, emotional/ psychological, financial and/or spiritual, and can include coercive control over a person's decisions and actions'.[7] This definition draws on project partner Lisa Oakley's definition of spiritual abuse as 'a form of emotional and psychological abuse ... characterised by a systematic pattern of coercive and controlling behaviour in a religious context' (2018: n.p.). These definitions of abuse are applicable across any religious context and are not limited to new religions. Indeed, most of the work for the Abuse in Religious Contexts project focuses on abuse in mainstream religions.

The issue of coercive control in religious movements, old and new, is a relatively fresh area of scholarly analysis (e.g. Blyth 2021), including in cultic and NRM studies.[8] Drawn from the field of domestic abuse and intimate partner violence, coercive control was described by Stark, who defines it as a form of 'entrapment' and 'subjugation' in which men 'dominate individual women by interweaving repeated physical abuse with three equally important tactics: intimidation, isolation and control' (2007: 23). Coercive control was

---

[7] https://blogs.ed.ac.uk/airc/about-the-project/.
[8] In cultic studies, Linda and Rob Dubrow-Marshall (who both hold various roles within ICSA) established an MSc in the Psychology of Coercive Control at the University of Salford following the criminalisation of coercive control in the UK Serious Crime Act (2015). This has marked a broadening of the field of cultic studies. For instance, in 2020, ICSA renamed its journal *The International Journal of Coercion, Manipulation and Abuse* (from *The International Journal of Cultic Studies*) and its scope includes not only cults but also domestic violence, trafficking, gangs and more. See www.ijcam.org/.

criminalised in the UK's Serious Crime Act (2015) and the Domestic Abuse Act (2021), where controlling behaviour is defined as 'a range of acts designed to make a person subordinate and/or dependent', and coercive behaviour is defined as 'a continuing act or a pattern of acts of assault, threats, humiliation and intimidation or other abuse that is used to harm, punish, or frighten their victim'. Legislation is limited to those in a current or previous intimate or family relationship. However, cult awareness groups such as The Family Survival Trust (FST) are campaigning for it to be extended to include relationships within religious movements. In their *Proposal for New Legislation* (2022), FST draws parallels between the mechanisms of coercive control and Lifton's eight principles of thought reform. FST sees coercive control as akin to brainwashing, calling for legislation that makes it 'a criminal offence to undertake the activities required to implement coercive control, thought reform, resocialisation, total conversion, mind control, brainwashing, bounded choice – or whatever term is the flavour of the day' (2022: 5). The resurgence of the discredited brainwashing narrative has angered NRM scholars who have dedicated decades of research to demonstrating that brainwashing, as it was conceptualised in cultic studies, does not exist and that current laws are sufficient for the prosecution of illegal behaviours to be found across all religious movements (Introvigne and Richardson 2022). Sessions and Doherty argue that 'the use of coercive control language in cultic studies is largely superficial and engages in tactical ambiguities which seek to apply various "cult brainwashing" ideas in a new context' (2023: 161). They recognise that there are similarities between coercive control tactics in intimate partner violence and NRMs, and that both fields can learn from each other, but they suggest that the conflation of coercive control with brainwashing is a concern – not least because coercive control needs to be justiciable.

Without conflating coercive control with brainwashing, I agree that coercive control can be considered a technique or mechanism of (largely gendered) abuse within religious movements. The tactics of coercive control, 'including threats, degradation, isolation, microregulation, surveillance, love-bombing, and gaslighting' (Blyth 2021: 4), are drawn out in the case study analysed in this Element. I agree with Jacobs that the patriarchal social structure of some NRMs has placed 'women and children especially at risk for violence and abuse' (2007: 234). I focus on the ways in which those with the least power – that is, women and children – are more likely to experience harm. But I recognise that gendered abuse intersects with other forms of abuse and that men too have been harmed in religious movements. Abuse includes not only specific instances of harm but also harmful environments, including the control of relationships and/or access to the outside world. Abuse can arise not only from direct forms of power that a religious leader holds over followers but also from the circulation of power within religious communities or families – the horizontal networks of member relationships, group norms and body disciplines. Orsi's (2019) conception of the shadow side or problematic elements of lived religion is pertinent here. He considers the ways in which embodied religious worlds are created from and contribute to unequal power relations, exclusivity, control and microregulation that can move into the realm of harm and abuse. I use a capacious understanding of abuse as a person's experience of harm resulting from imbalances of power in relationships within a religious context and I analyse specific structural and cultural factors which could result in an experience of harm. These factors, and the case study which illustrates them, are drawn from NRM studies, but the factors can also be identified in established mainstream religious traditions. This is not a model exclusively for analysing abuse in new religions, even if some of the structural factors might be more likely to be found there.

## 2 A Theoretical Model of Abuse: Structural and Cultural Factors

In this section I introduce a theoretical model of abuse consisting of six structural factors and six cultural factors. This list contributes to the development of a theoretical model for analysing factors which might contribute to the perpetration of abuse, to the legitimisation of abuse, to the propensity not to investigate abuse or only to investigate internally, without involving external agencies. However, a number of caveats are needed. First, these factors should not be considered a checklist; their presence in a religious movement does not mean that abuse *will* occur but rather that a combination of some of them *might* enable harmful and abusive situations. Hence, they are not predictive factors. They are features that can make people more vulnerable to abuse but there will also be other, non-religious elements at play, including individual circumstances, relationships with family, with other social structures, external sources of support or lack thereof. Religion should not be looked at in isolation from other social structures. Nor is it a list of cult characteristics by which religious movements with these factors can be defined as cults. These aspects can be found across all forms of religious movements, as survivor testimonies from those who have experienced abuse in the Anglican and Catholic churches highlight. Some of these features are also found in non-religious organisations and institutions. However, some components are connected to the organisation and internal culture of new religious movements, including separation from society (structurally and/or ideologically), charismatic leadership and the enthusiasm of first generation converts which has consequences for the degree of willing submission to authority. While there is nothing unique about abuse in

NRMs, nor is it necessarily more likely to occur here, NRMs can be considered as small social experiments on the margins of society. They therefore provide insights as to how controversies are constructed and managed in other areas of society (Beckford 1985).

The structural factors are as follows:

1. Isolation – the group's relationship with wider society and whether members are physically or socially isolated. Do members live communally? Is their access and connection to the outside world restricted in any way?
2. Leadership – forms of leadership, particularly charismatic authority. Does the leader have absolute authority within the group? A divine status? Are there punishments for disobeying his/her authority? Over what aspects of life does this authority extend?
3. Membership – relationships within the group including whether there is a hierarchy of members. Is there an inner circle of members who have a special status, are considered closer to the leader and/or more spiritually adept? What are the interactions between different levels?
4. Blurred Boundaries – are strong boundaries with the outside world accompanied by blurred boundaries around roles and responsibilities within the group? That is, is there no distinction into different spheres of life and different types of interpersonal relations? Are these (lack of) boundaries policed and micro-regulated?
5. Education – whether the group provides its own educational system for members' children. Does it separate children from their parents and/or from the wider society? Is children's education restricted in any way?
6. Health – whether the group provides its own health system for members and/or encourages them to seek alternatives to allopathic medicine. Does it promote alternative healing methods or healing in a ritualistic context? Are there healers within the movement who are favoured over external sources?

These structural factors are supported by the movement's religious teachings, considered here as cultural factors. These are:

1. Unequivocal beliefs – teachings around the superiority, exclusivity or the unique legitimacy of the group. Is an us/them dichotomy created, a culture of in-group superiority? Are members distinguished from outsiders, including through specific terminology?
2. Gender – are teachings around gender relations justified through religious texts and embodied through group norms and practices? Is one gender

considered superior? Or are the genders ostensibly 'equal but different' which still leads to restrictions on one more than the other?
3. Sex – are teachings around sexual relationships justified through texts and embodied through practices which are controlled through forms of micro-regulation? Are practices policed? Are there ritual practices around sex?
4. Purification – are teachings around purity and purification, not only of individual members but also of the group itself, linked to concerns with salvation and with the superiority and selectivity of the group?
5. Punishments and pressures – are there (spiritual) consequences for disobedience or for dissent? What role do other members play in policing? Are forms of confession practised, such as group sharing of sins and transgressions? Are these then held against members, used as blackmail or for coercive control?
6. Leaving and shunning – are there barriers and high exit costs to leaving the movement, or more formal mechanisms of shunning, exclusion or disfellowshipping?

It should be noted that this division into structural and cultural factors – considered here as the movement's organisational structure and interactions with society, on the one hand, and its religious teachings, on the other – is an artificial distinction. In reality, and as the following discussion emphasises, the factors are intertwined in various ways. For example, it is not easy to analyse a movement's degree of social isolation without understanding its teachings around exclusivity and unique legitimacy. In the remainder of this section, I focus on four groupings of these factors to show how structural and cultural factors are intertwined and best analysed in interactions with one another. These groupings are: (1) a movement's relationship with wider society, including whether members are physically or socially isolated, and its teachings on unique legitimacy, exclusivity and superiority; (2) authority structures including forms of leadership, membership hierarchies and blurred boundaries between different spheres of life and interpersonal relations; (3) teachings on gender and sex and their regulation, including body disciplines, purity practices and health and healing practices; and (4) forms of punishment, threats and pressures, including whether there are spiritual consequences for disobedience or for dissent and whether there are barriers and high exit costs to leaving the movement.

## Isolation and Unique Legitimacy

Definitions of cult, sect and NRM all hinge on their relationship with wider society and dominant religious traditions. All three terms suggest a religious movement that is in some way in tension with societal norms. Barker suggests that tension with society arises from the characteristics associated with a first generation of converts, including the enthusiasm with which members hold their beliefs, leaders' desires to keep members separate from the world in order to protect those beliefs, and a dichotomous worldview in which people are divided into members and non-members (2004: 94). Although these are not necessarily features of concern, forms of isolation and the mechanisms to enforce them can be contributing factors in abuse. It is important to recognise, however, both a movement's propensity to change and different forms and degrees of isolation. All religious movements have some degree of interaction with society which may increase or decrease over time, with the typical trajectory being *increasing* engagement as second and subsequent generations energise a movement (Barker 2014; van Eck Duymaer van Twist 2015). Increased interaction with society can lessen the propensity for abuse, due to increased opportunities for and access to external sources of support and oversight and to accountability structures. However, this is in many ways an over-simplification, as abuses within the socially integrated Church of England highlight.

In the 1980s, a number of scholars developed NRM typologies based on movements' relationships with wider society. Wallis (1984) created a typology based on 'orientations to the world': that is, whether movements were world-accommodating, world-rejecting or world-affirming. Beckford (1985), on the other hand, argued that even world-rejecting movements had to engage in the 'political and moral economies' of wider society, and developed a more complex framework of 'modes of insertion'. He outlined 'the variety of ways in which NRMs are related to their social environments' (1985: 76), including relationships internal to NRMs and external relationships between NRMs and wider society. Beckford's three-fold typology of refuge, revitalization and release, bears similarity to Wallis's typology of 'orientations to the world', but with greater attention on how and why a movement interacts with the outside world. It is the refuge, like the world-rejecting NRM, which is the quintessential type in the popular imagination, with members living as separate from the world as possible in order to maintain 'the purity/impurity boundary' (Beckford 1985: 85). However, Beckford suggests that historically utopian religious communities have not been controversial (1985: 118); rather, they may become so in 'their attempts to find a location in society as agents of transformation or release' (1985: 119). It is, then, in their very engagement with society that they become controversial. This is true to some extent: it was interaction with external sources which led to the deviance amplification spiral that ended in the mass deaths of members at both Jonestown in 1978 and Waco in 1993, for example. But these communities had already created harmful environments for some members even before their tragic ends.

Communal living is not inherently problematic (Miller 2013), but it can be if other factors are also at play. One issue which has proved controversial in a number of NRMs is the treatment of children, particularly in movement-run boarding schools in which children were separated from their parents. A movement's relationship with education can intersect with isolation and unique legitimacy in multifaceted ways. Some groups have created their own education systems, which are either reserved for members or marketed to non-members as a superior form of education. Others send their children to secular state schools but exclude their children from the full range of opportunities that are available. Children might be withdrawn from extra-curricular activities, sports or Religious Education lessons, for such reasons as being too worldly, or contrary to religious principles, and hence inappropriate. This can be accompanied by a de-valuing of secular education for being part of the outside world. Some former members have reported that though they did receive a state education, the discouragement and lack of value placed on continuing into tertiary education limited their educational horizon and career opportunities (Ploeg 2017).

It has also been argued that children who are educated only within a particular religious worldview might not be considered to receive an 'efficient' education,[9] leaving them ill-prepared if they do leave that religious community (Bloom 2023; Fletcher 2023). Polarised positions exist as to whether this should be considered abuse but certainly children will not have had all the opportunities and experiences that are available to their peers, although they will have had others.[10] Educational systems can be a factor which enables abuse in religious movements when children are separated from parents, when staff have inadequate training, when there is little oversight or inspection by external authorities, and when the physical environment is unsafe. In several cases children have experienced emotional, physical and sexual abuse in boarding schools or educational settings run by NRMs, including the International Society for Krishna Consciousness (ISKCON) (Rochford and Heinlein 1998), Children of God (COG)/The Family International (TFI) (van Eck Duymaer van Twist 2015; Barker 2022) and 3HO (Deslippe and Stukin 2020). For example, Rochford and Heinlein (1998), describing ISKCON's *gurukulas* (boarding

---

[9] The UK's 1996 Education Act states that children must 'receive efficient full-time education ... either by regular attendance at school or otherwise' (section 7). It does not define 'efficient'.

[10] The literature on parents' rights to educate children in their religious faith, including religious schooling, is vast. It is a contested area, being a particular focus of the New Atheist movement characterised by Richard Dawkins who has compared religious education to a form of child abuse (2006). Some NRM scholars, on the other hand, have noted the different opportunities and experiences that an alternative education provides, attending to particularities and to lived experiences (Palmer 2016; Pratezina 2019).

schools) in the 1970s and 1980s, outlined the ways in which structural and cultural factors combined to create situations in which children were not theologically valued within a movement which placed celibate males at the apex of a spiritual hierarchy. Children were instead seen as a hindrance to adults' paths to salvation, while, for adults, working in the *gurukulas* was seen as a demeaning role. Such work was sometimes used as a punishment for adults not meeting their missionary targets, meaning that there was a high turnover of ill-trained staff. The *gurukulas* became 'defined by neglect, isolation and marginalization' (Rochford and Heinlein 1998: 53). In 2000, around forty survivors of the *gurukulas* filed a lawsuit in a federal court in Dallas against ISKCON for the abuse they had suffered (Children of ISKCON v. ISKCON 2000). The case concluded in 2008, with ISKCON paying out $15 million in settlements and legal fees.[11] ISKCON has since instituted reforms in its organisational and educational structure and no longer advocates separating children from their parents into boarding schools. However, some adults, who were abused as children in the *gurukulas* have expressed anger that some of the perpetrators have been sheltered by the movement and never held fully accountable for their actions (van Eck Duymaer van Twist 2015: 55–9).

Movements do not have to practise communal living for all members, or educate children within the movement, to promote forms of social isolation. Different members within the same movement have different experiences. Some movements have a core group of devotees who live communally, for example, the Church of Scientology's Sea Organization ('Sea Org'), Jehovah's Witnesses who live at Bethel and JFC members who were part of the New Creation Christian Community, while the majority of members live in society at large. Those who live in community will likely be more socially isolated than those who live in the world. This can partly be an incidental or practical factor, as day-to-day life does not leave time for engagement with wider society, but it can also be more ideological, motivated by policing the boundaries of membership. This is pronounced in some new Christian movements, including Jehovah's Witnesses, JFC and the Plymouth Brethren Christian Church, which have not created physical refuges but do consider themselves holy societies separate from the world. This obligation of separation affects members' daily lives as their individual holiness contributes to the holiness or purity of the organisation. In this way, an NRM's separation from society is never purely structural; it is religiously justified with claims of unique legitimacy, superiority, and exclusivity. Of course, it could be argued that *all* religious

---

[11] See the timeline of the case on the website of ex-member Nori Muster, https://surrealist.org/gurukula/timeline/lawsuit.html.

movements make some kind of claim to unique truth, but when considering issues of abuse, there is relevance in the degree to which these claims are made, the mechanisms to enforce them and the extent to which this creates an us-and-them dichotomy.

One means through which a movement maintains social isolation and unique legitimacy is through restricting relationships between members and non-members. This is suggested in the creation of Christian holy societies, where non-members might be engaged with only for the purposes of proselytization. This can create difficulties in families where some individuals are part of a religious group, while others are not. Sometimes a convert to an NRM can temporarily cut off contact with family and friends, because they are in a honeymoon period, and dedicating all of their time and energy to the new movement, leaving no time for previous contacts and interests (Barker 1989). However, some movements explicitly encourage disconnecting from relatives and friends, especially when they are critical. Distinctions between members and non-members can be reinforced through language, such as labelling systems. For example, some Christian groups refer to those on the outside as 'worldlies' (JFC) or 'systemites' (COG/TFI).[12] This reinforces boundaries and a sense of in-group superiority, exclusion from which can contribute to an individual's feeling of isolation, while inclusion can effect a lack of alternative perspectives and close off external sources of support.[13]

Oakley (2018) and others have noted that survivors of religious abuse can experience isolation within their movements once they disclose their abuse experience, whether they disclose to someone within the movement or outside of it. Isolation then can also be connected to disclosure. Not only does lack of engagement with wider society reduce an individual's ability to disclose but it can also increase the chances of negative responses from others within the movement and transpire in a propensity to only investigate claims internally. The 2021 investigation report of the Independent Inquiry into Child Sexual Abuse (IICSA) outlines numerous barriers to reporting child sexual abuse which include 'distrust of external agencies'.[14] The IICSA report includes

---

[12] It should also be noted that the use of jargon has been included in definitions of cult that build on Lifton's principle of 'loading the language', one of his eight principles of 'thought reform' (1961). See Montell (2021) for a more recent analysis of 'the linguistic elements that make a wide spectrum of communities cultish'.

[13] For this reason, Inform recommends that relatives stay in touch with loved ones in an NRM; see https://inform.ac/guidelines-for-friends-family/.

[14] The Independent Inquiry into Child Sexual Abuse was a statutory inquiry which ran from 2015–2022 and comprised fifteen investigations into institutionalised child abuse. A number of minority religions were included in its *Child protection in religious organisations and settings: Investigation report* (2021). There has been some criticism of this report's analysis of the Jehovah's Witnesses 'two witness' rule (Introvigne 2021a).

testimony from a former JFC member and from former Witnesses which suggest that, in their cases, distrust was linked to a sense of religious superiority and exclusivity (2021: 32). IICSA also notes that Jehovah's Witnesses 'do not draw on any external assistance' in developing child protection policies because, as the Witness representative explained, their policies are considered 'a religious application of Bible principles' (2021: 54). There is a lack of engagement with external, secular organisations, as they are considered inferior sources of authority compared with biblical principles.

An organisation's relationship with society is important to consider not just in terms of its propensity to create abusive environments but also in terms of how it responds to abuse allegations. Many NRMs practise forms of social isolation, to a greater or lesser degree, to protect their social and moral boundaries. This does not mean that they are necessarily more prone to abuse but that they can construct barriers to reporting abuse, not least because of distrust towards external agencies as being of the world and therefore hostile to them. Lack of engagement with external organisations can reduce a religious movement's accountability structures, leading to practices of dealing with allegations internally only, which frequently serves to protect the organisation and abusers within it at the expense of the abused individual (IICSA 2021).

## Authority Structures

Abuse, perpetrated through an unequal power dynamic, cannot be understood outside of authority structures. In religious movements this includes relationships of authority and submission between leaders and followers. As Oakley and Humphreys note, abuse is not only perpetrated by leaders in religious contexts – religious leaders can be victims of abuse too (2019: 7–8, 111). But abuse by a leader, or an individual in a position of religious authority over another, is a more common scenario. Abuse can occur under different forms of religious leadership (Weber 1922) and power (French and Raven 1959; Lukes 2004). The institutional authority of clergy, and its weaponisation in the legitimation and concealment of abuse, has been a major area of study (Shupe 1995, 2007; Shupe, Stacey and Darnell 2000; Keenan 2012; Scorer 2014; Oakley and Humphreys 2019). A deference to religious authority can be an enabling factor in abuse, particularly when authority is legitimised through claims to a unique connection with the divine. It is arguably in charismatic authority – the form of authority most associated with NRMs (Barker 2004; Prophet 2016) – where the strongest claims to divine leadership are made. Furthermore, the characteristics of charismatic authority, and the form of relationship it encourages between the charismatic leader and their followers, can be an enabling factor in abuse.

Charismatic authority is characterised by its lack of accountability. As such, it 'operates outside the norms of rational society' (Hofmann and Dawson 2014: 350), drawing its authority not from tradition or rules but from the qualities *perceived* to reside in the charismatic individual figure. Weber defined charisma as 'a certain quality of an individual personality by virtue of which he is set apart from ordinary men and treated as endowed with supernatural, superhuman, or at least specifically exceptional powers or qualities' (1968: 241). These powers or qualities are not within the remit of ordinary people but instead are believed to be of divine origin, and it is on this basis that 'the individual concerned is treated as a leader' (1968: 241). The charismatic leader frequently has a messianic or divine status or at least is believed to have unique access to divine truth and answers to salvation. As such, they are beyond questioning and challenge if they abuse their position of authority.

Charisma must be recognised in the individual for it to be authoritative. It is in processes of charismatisation (Barker 1993) – through which demonstrations of charisma such as healing or divine visions are accepted and relayed – that new followers learn of the individual's status and significance from others. In this, it is inherently relational and relies on relationships of trust and emotion between followers and leader, regardless of whether there are direct personal connections. Furthermore, the charismatic leader's authority frequently extends beyond the religious life to govern all aspects of followers' lives. Barker describes how members of the Unification Church (UC) believed that Rev Moon 'has a legitimate right to tell them where and at what to work and how to live', that he is 'capable of choosing the right marriage partner for them' and that some 'have been prepared to leave their children at his behest' (1993: 187). The process of charismatisation, through which Moon acquires the authority and legitimacy to make these mandates, hinges on two additional factors, Barker suggests. These are the UC's 'relatively closed environment, in which outside influences are kept to a minimum' (1993: 190) and its 'relatively authoritarian environment' in which the convert is 'subject to constant pressure both from their leaders … and from their peers' (1993: 191).[15] Charismatic authority can thus be linked to a movement's practice of isolation and to blurred boundaries and regulation of members' lives.

A further characteristic of charismatic authority relevant to its propensity to enable abuse is its gendered nature. The intersections of gender and charismatic authority remain under-theorised. NRM scholars have attempted to refocus the gender imbalance by highlighting the many instances of female charismatic

---

[15] Barker was writing about the Unification Church in the 1980s and 1990s and, following the death of Moon in 2012, these statements no longer apply to the current movement.

authority within new religions (Wessinger 1993; Palmer 1994; Vance 2015; Prophet 2017). Jacobs (1989) was one of the first NRM scholars to take a critical feminist perspective, arguing that women left NRMs because of their unfulfilled expectations of male charismatic leaders. Female members thereby participated in an 'economy of love' in which they demonstrated devotion and submission to the male leader and, through him, to the divine, in return for love and affection from the male leader and, mediated by him, the divine realm. This situation lent itself to exploitation and abuse. Lucia (2018) has suggested a framework of 'haptic logics' for understanding the guru-disciple relationship and the way in which charismatic authority is maintained. She suggests that followers partake in the guru's sacred status through touch, including massage and other forms of embodied care, which casts them in a feminised role. Followers' desire, encouragement and obligations for close physical proximity and touch with their leader, to partake in their sacredness, is frequently gendered and sometimes subject to abuse. Haptic logics provide the social context not only for sexual abuse but also 'creates serious barriers to the vindication of victims' (2018: 955).

Other scholars have argued that Weber's very definitions of authority are masculine-biased. Joosse and Willey note that 'charisma appears as a masculine property and its bestowal is tantamount to masculinization' (2020: 6). As they intimate, and others have discussed more explicitly (Feuchtwang 2008; Lloyd 2018), new theorisations of charisma broaden the understanding beyond the divine origin assumption and include discussions of whether it is possible to distinguish between good and bad charisma. Feuchtwang states that 'good charisma is surely accountable charisma' (2008: 104); Lloyd makes a similar distinction between authoritarian and democratic forms of charisma (2018: 3–4). Authoritarian charisma, he argues, is based on seduction which itself is gendered (2018: 9). It is the charisma associated 'with fathers, with law, and with enchantment' (2018: 6). In contrast to democratic charisma, which has the potential for emancipation, authoritarian charisma 'naturalizes injustice' (2018: 24) and conceals violence, including sexual violence. It is then specifically *authoritarian* charisma which has the potential to enable and to conceal abuse.

Some NRM scholars (Chryssides 2021; Richardson 2021) have argued that too much emphasis has been placed on the individual figure of the charismatic leader as an explanation for the creation of NRMs and for member recruitment and retention. Richardson argues that the 'myth of the omnipotent leader' exists in a pairing with the 'myth of the passive and brainwashed follower', which eradicates the agency of those who choose to join and remain in new religions. The high attrition rates of new religions negate these myths. Richardson also discusses cases in which followers exerted 'control over leaders who are perceived to have misused their leadership positions and caused harm to the group and its members' (2021: 14). As noted above, it is not only leaders who harm followers.

It is also important to be attentive to the circulation of power within different relationships, and how expectations, pressures and norms within horizontal relationships can become authoritative, including the role played by an inner circle of members in charismatisation (the 'charismatic aristocracy' in Weber's terminology, or the 'charisma of the cadre' in Moore's [2021]). Established members maintain the charismatic authority of the leader and socialise new members into the movement. This is not an abusive practice, not least because not all charismatic leaders abuse their followers. But for leaders who *are* abusive, an inner circle of members can become complicit, as was the case in the violence encouraged by Jim Jones of Peoples Temple and Shoko Asahara of Aum Shinrikyo (Moore 2021). Teachings around gender and sexual relationships can entwine with charismatic authority and membership hierarchies, highlighting the interaction of structural and cultural factors.

Hierarchical authority structures can be justified by the religious movement's teachings and texts creating further potentialities for their use in the legitimisation of abuse. As Oakley and Humphreys note, the problem of spiritual abuse was initially identified in Christian churches with a practice of discipling or 'heavy shepherding' (2019: 5). Based on scripture such as the book of Acts, discipling or shepherding is a model of authority and submission in which spiritually mature Christians teach, counsel and discipline those newer to the faith. In new Christian movements, such as house churches, the discipler's authority frequently extends beyond religious counsel to encompass all areas of life, including dating and relationships, family structures and childcare, and careers and leisure time. As the discipler's authority is based on their religious standing and qualities, they often have no external training around leadership or counselling and no checks and balances by others. This creates the potential for controlling relationships, either as a direct result of the abuse of the position of authority or as a more indirect complicity in the structure which can lead to micro-regulation of members' lives and their experience of pressure to conform. Intricately linked to both charismatic authority and hierarchical membership is the all-encompassing nature of membership in some new religions.

Cultic studies organisations, such as ICSA, have used terms such as 'high demand groups' and 'totalism' (Lifton 1961) in order to categorise movements which control members, who in turn express complete dedication, enthusiasm and submission to authority. Such movements are not only religious but also include political, environmental, sports and fitness, health and wellbeing and online movements (Montell 2021). Some NRM scholars, such as Wessinger (2008), have rejected the use of these terms as categorising or boundary-marker terms, marking some religious movements as totalistic and others not. They advocate recognising that all social movements exist on a continuum of totalism, and that identifying totalistic characteristics can be a useful framework for analysing potential moves to violence. As Wessinger notes, 'When assessing whether a social group poses danger to members and outsiders, it is best to include a determination of the degree to which it possesses totalistic characteristics' (2008: n.p.). These characteristics centre on the relationships between leader(s) and followers. Bromley (2011) identifies totalism as one of the internal factors which can contribute to violence perpetrated by NRMs, other factors being millennialism and charismatic leadership. However, totalism can have multiple meanings: it can refer not only to the creation of a totalistic environment, as described above, applicable to any organisation, but it can also refer to making a totalising claim over one's whole life, salvation and ultimate reality, and it is then more applicable to the religious context.

It is in this sense that abuse in a religious context can have an additional dimension. As Oakley and Humphreys (2019) note, spiritual abuse not only incorporates spiritual elements into the abuse, such as the weaponisation of scripture but also affects the individual's spiritual life and their relationship with the divine. I suggest that both forms of totalism can be conceptualised with the term 'blurred boundaries': the control of members' lives through structures of authority and submission, and the totalistic claims the religious movement makes on one's life and salvation. In situations of blurred boundaries, there is no distinction into different spheres of life and different types of interpersonal relations. It is more than simply identifying a situation as high-demand, which can be difficult to define and is often focused on time commitments, such as Montell's suggestion that religious movements are 'healthy' when they stick to 'ritual time' and do not permeate all areas of life (2021: 125). Blurred boundaries are a characteristic which can be found to varying degrees across all religious movements, rather than a definition of one type of religious movement. They are also a factor which can contribute to the abuse of members.

The characteristics of NRMs noted by Barker (2004), stemming from the enthusiasm of a first generation of converts and their charismatic leader's control over all aspects of their lives, contribute to creating a situation of blurred boundaries. In movements in which the member's whole life is entwined with the NRM, unclear and fuzzy boundaries can come to characterise interpersonal relationships, distinctions between the religious movement and employment and living arrangements, time and financial commitments, and private and public spaces, including one's own bodily boundaries. This has multiple implications for the potential for abuse to arise, including the micro-regulation of members' lives and the high exit costs of leaving such a movement. In practical terms, it is difficult to leave a movement for which one also works, because one might be financially dependent; or the movement might provide the accommodation where one lives, and it might constitute the orbit where one's friends and family are. This is even more pronounced for those born and raised within socially and/or physically isolated religious movements (van Eck Duymaer van Twist 2015).

Blurred boundaries are intricately connected to structures of authority and submission and issues of control. Members' lives in NRMs with blurred boundaries can be policed and micro-regulated, not only directly by leaders but also indirectly by peers in the creation of group pressures, norms and bodily disciplines to conform to certain lifestyles. It can be every aspect of a member's being which is under such pressures, with authority extending beyond the religious, spiritual or pastoral domain to include occupation, leisure, family, social and financial life.[16] Such a situation is not confined to any single religious tradition but the discipling structure and communal living arrangements of some Christian movements can exacerbate this factor, as the JFC case demonstrates. These structures can also contribute to difficulties with disclosing abuse when the obligation is to disclose to one's discipler, an individual implicated in the authority structure of the movement. Lawsuits brought by survivors of abuse in the International Churches of Christ (ICOC) detail the connection between the practice of discipling and the micro-regulation of all aspects of life (Borecka 2023), as do a number of allegations against other new Christian movements, including SPAC Nation (White and Youle 2019; Bloom 2023: 137–8) and the Universal Church of the Kingdom of God (McClenaghan 2022). These cases illustrate the ways in which it can be those in the lowest positions in the hierarchy who are subject to the most regulation, control and pressures to conform. Frequently, there are classed and gendered aspects to this factor.

## Teachings on Gender and Sex

A further form of authority structure in religious movements is their teachings on gender and sex and the regulation of these through interpersonal relationships, body disciplines and other practices including those concerning purity and healing. Such teachings can contribute to experiences of harm and abuse when they legitimise environments in which women are treated as inferior to men and/or they directly legitimise the sexual abuse of women. Such teachings also play a role in experiences of disclosure in situations where women have to

---

[16] I recognise that this division into different spheres of life, and the possibility of separating the religious life from other spheres, is a normative position resulting from secular, Westernised, contemporary scholarship.

report experiences of abuse to male elders. This is because they often run concurrent with other authority structures, such as discipling structures or the authoritarian charisma that a male leader holds over his female and/or feminised followers.

Women are more likely to experience abuse than men in all sectors of society, not only in religious movements and, in this sense, there is nothing anomalous or unique about religion. Gender-based abuse or violence, abuse perpetrated against another person because of their actual or perceived gender, is more likely to be experienced by women and girls, who are generally more at risk of domestic violence, rape and sexual abuse, and honour-based abuse. Women are also more likely to be victims of gendered techniques of abuse such as coercive control (Stark 2007; Anderson 2009) and gaslighting, which employ tactics that 'are gendered in that they rely on the association of femininity with irrationality' (Sweet 2019: 851). These forms of gendered abuse are found in families where religion may be a factor in the domestic abuse of women and children (Nason-Clark 2000, 2003; Afzal and Stiebert 2024), and/or they can be played out in the dynamics of religious leaders and followers or among peers in religious movements. What can make abuse in a religious context different is the use of religious texts, teachings, norms and practices, and the weight of spiritual authority these carry, to legitimise abuse.

As small innovative movements with beliefs and practices different from the mainstream, NRMs have been sites of gender and sex experimentation, from eighteenth-century communes advocating celibacy (such as the Shakers), to nineteenth-century communes advocating free love (such as the Oneida Perfectionists), to twenty-first-century human potential and neo-Tantric groups advocating sex as a technique of enlightenment (such as Osho) (Palmer 1994; Urban 2003; Wilcox 2011). Some scholars have argued that NRMs offer alternative religious roles for women, including greater opportunities for leadership, not least because they are based on alternative sources of authority. The preponderance of women, as both practitioners and leaders, in Esoteric, Pagan, New Age and holistic spiritualities is often given as evidence for the empowering roles that women might find in these forms of religious movements (McGuire 2003; Heelas and Woodhead 2005; Sointu and Woodhead 2008; Vance 2015). Others have argued that some women choose to join new religions specifically because of their ideals of patriarchal authority, discrete gender roles and support for the traditional family – ideals that are believed to be lacking, or under attack, in contemporary Western societies (e.g. Dawson 2000). This might be the case for some converts to new Christian movements which hold conservative views of marriage and sexual relationships. However, it would be a gross over-simplification to suggest that women who uphold normative gender values join traditional religious movements and hence experience a degree of oppression and abuse, whereas women who desire gender equality join alternative religious movements and hence experience empowerment. The lived reality is always more complex, not least because empowerment is a 'slippery' and subjective concept (Palmer 1994: 8). Not only do women negotiate their positions and sense of power in groups in which they are marginalised (Ammerman 1987; Palmer 1994; Inge 2016), including through their relationships with the male leader (Maaga 1998), but there are also experiences of abuse in women-led new religions (such as Church Universal and Triumphant, Prophet 2018). Puttick argues that most NRMs replicate male hegemony and have continued a social subordination of women, despite some examples of doctrinal gender equality and 'experimentation around sexuality and family structures' (1997: 152).

A pervasive view of gender relations across all sectors of society is that there are two genders aligned with two biological sexes, which dictate the roles, responsibilities and characteristics associated with each. This has been termed complementarian theology within the Christian context, but it is also found across religious traditions, including the other Abrahamic faiths (Judaism and Islam) and South Asian-based religions (Hinduism and Buddhism), where religious doctrines of gender equality have often been constrained by patriarchal cultures. Of course, other doctrines of gender relations can be found in religions, including movements which see the gendered body 'as a superficial layer of false identity obscuring the immortal, sexless spirit' (Palmer 1994: 10, who gives the examples of Scientology, the Raelians and various human potential groups). These doctrines, too, might enable abuse, yet it is arguably complementarian theology which can legitimise specifically gender-based forms of abuse.

Religious teachings around gender relations do not remain on a theological, abstract level but are rather enacted through practice, specifically through interpersonal relationships and sexual activity. It is arguably through teachings on sex that gender relations are most strongly embodied and enacted. Sexual practice is important in religious movements because it maintains the boundaries of the group, not just literally, through the creation of the next generation, but also metaphorically in terms of how sexual practice might determine membership, who is included and excluded, and the religious significance of the next generation. This factor is then sometimes linked to a movement's teachings on unique legitimacy. In the Unification Church, for instance, Rev Moon taught that God's kingdom of heaven on earth could be restored through the creation of 'blessed families'. Through ritual practices around marriage ('the Blessing') and consummation (the 'Holy Wine Ceremony'), 'fallen nature' (original sin) could be eradicated in the next generation. This 'pure' next generation of 'blessed children' were of special significance in the movement's theology, with a unique role to play in its eschatology (van Eck Duymaer van Twist 2015). Ritual practices around sex are not inherently problematic but some scholars (Nevalainen 2011) and former members (Hong 1998; Barlow 2017) of the UC have noted controversial aspects of this practice. In the early days of the movement, Moon is reported to have engaged in ritual practices in which he purified women's wombs through sexual intercourse (Nevalainen 2011).[17]

As suggested above, NRMs have been sites of experimentation of gender roles and sexual practices. Forms of ritualised sex include The Great Rite performed in some Wiccan groups, Esoteric sex magic practices, Hindu and Buddhist *karmamudra* or consort teachings, and neo-Tantric sexual practice in order to reach enlightenment. These are important religious practices for many consenting adults, and it is not for the religious studies scholar to take a normative position and label them good or bad sexual practices. Goodwin (2020) has outlined the dangers of equating alternative sexual practices with abuse and with using this equation to discriminate against new and minority religious movements. She traces the ways in which an 'incorrect but tenacious assumption' has been created in American society 'that religious difference causes sexual abuse' (2020: 1). Goodwin argues that horror stories about sexual violence in minority religions, perpetuated in the media and in popular books, have served to limit American religious and sexual difference, creating a normative culture of 'contraceptive nationalism ... a form of gendered white supremacist Christian nativism' (2020: 3). This is because it is intertwined with 'captivity narratives' in which white women and children are framed as needing rescuing from sexually abusive religious and/or ethnic 'others'.[18] However, it is important to look at the specific instances when sexual practices have been reported as abusive in order to consider how specific teachings on gender and sex can be an enabling or legitimising factor in abuse. This is often when sexual practices move into the realms of pressure and coercive control, bolstered by unequal power relations and the authority of religious texts and teachings.

Abuse has occurred in NRMs with vastly different teachings on sex on a permissive to conservative spectrum. Movements with permissive sexual

---

[17] According to Nevalainen, these were *pikareun* rituals – a Korean shamanic practice of purifying the womb and allowing a change of blood lineage. However, it should be noted that Nevalainen's claims are disputed by other scholars, see https://www.cesnur.org/2014/sexmoon.htm.

[18] This is different from Bromley's (1998: 154) conception of the 'captivity narrative' as a story told by 'apostates' to justify their joining and then renouncing their religious movement, and warning others of its dangers, often through the anticult movement.

practices, which see sexual activity as part of the spiritual path, sexual intercourse as a re-enactment of the divine, and sex as akin to meditation or a mystical state, include Pagan, Esoteric, neo-Tantric and some Hindu and Buddhist groups as noted above. Osho was an important twentieth-century figure who popularised this view of sex and religion,[19] as was Aleister Crowley in the late nineteenth/ early twentieth-century, drawing on Western Esotericism and interpretations of Asian traditions. But permissive sexuality has also been central to some new Christian movements, most notably the Children of God, which later became The Family International. An evangelical movement with roots in the Jesus People movement of 1960s America, its founder David Berg (1919–1994) taught the Law of Love as foundational to the movement. His expression of love for God and for others included sexual activity manifested, in the 1970s, in the practice of Flirty Fishing. In this practice, women used sex as a form of witnessing – reaching out to the fish (most often men) through sex. But alongside this permissive sexuality and free love among consenting adults, there were also instances of abuse. Female former members have described pressure to engage in sexual relations as soon as they joined the movement, including with older men (Jones, Jones and Buhring 2008). These sexual practices also served to reinforce traditional, heteronormative gender roles as it was women who performed the role of 'fishers of men', while still fulfilling the sexual needs of their partners and, given the movement's rejection of contraception, often having a larger than average number of children. This social context created a difficult environment for some children born within the movement, given large family sizes, frequent moves between mission fields and the collective 'home education' of children (van Eck Duymaer van Twist 2015). There were also cases of child sexual abuse as the Law of Love allowed for sexual intercourse with children for a time (Melton 1994: 83). Berg's teachings on sex were an enabling factor in abuse in numerous ways – from directly legitimating certain practices to creating enabling social environments.

Movements which have advocated celibacy have also not been without problems. Distinctions can be made between movements which advocate celibacy for religious leaders (such as the Catholic Church and some Hindu and Buddhist groups), to those where it is advocated for some members (the practice of *brahmacharya* in some Hindu groups such as ISKCON), to those where it is

---

[19] And about whom there have been allegations of abuse (Puttick 1997) including in the Netflix documentary, *Children of the Cult* (2024), which itself grew out of former member dissatisfaction that abuse allegations were not covered in the previous Netflix documentary, *Wild, Wild Country* (2018). See e.g. www.theguardian.com/film/2024/oct/02/children-of-the-cult-review-osho-commune-bhagwan-shree-rajneesh-wild-wild-country.

an option for any member (such as in the JFC, where celibacy was held as the ideal for all although only practised by a minority). In some movements, celibacy might not be explicitly encouraged but the single man is still placed at the apex of the spiritual hierarchy. In a minority of movements, it is same-sex relationships which are advocated as the ideal. Although not a formal teaching, former members of the Friends of the Western Buddhist Order – which became the Triratna Buddhist Order – have claimed that this was an implicit teaching for a time within the movement. Founder Sangharakshita (Dennis Lingwood, 1925–2018) moved from a celibate monk to a non-celibate Head of Order and had a number of sexual relationships with male students in the 1960s to 1980s (Adhisthana Kula 2020: 10–11, 19). Some of these men later reported that they felt pressured into these relationships (2020: 10).[20] Some had been led to believe that sexual relationships were an aspect of 'spiritual friendship' (*kalyana mitrata*) and engaged in these relationships for this reason when they might not otherwise have done so (2020: 20–1).[21] The Adhisthana Kula report also states that other teachers copied Sangharakshita's sexual behaviour and that there was no recognition of the power imbalance between teachers and students and the impact of this on relationships (2020: 12). When Sangharakshita returned to a position of celibacy in the late 1980s, the report suggests, celibacy became favoured within the movement. It states that 'problematic ideas' within the movement, in addition to sex as spiritual friendship, included assertions that 'Male homosexuality is spiritually superior to heterosexuality; Men are spiritually superior to women; Single people are spiritually superior to those in relationships or families' (2020: 17). For a time, a spiritual hierarchy was created based on gender relations and sexual practices. It is important to look at a movement's specific teachings on sex and gender but it is also possible to identify commonalities around power relations, the authority of texts and teachers, pressures, and group norms and expectations. Abuse always derives from a power imbalance and, in reality, even groups with radical expressions of equality and free love often replicate imbalanced gender relations (Jacobs 1989; Puttick 1997).

A further means through which gender inequalities are embodied and sexuality policed are in religious practices around purity and purification. These are inherently linked to the gendered and sexed body as women's bodies and their

---

[20] In 2016 Sangharakshita made a 'confession', without going into details, apologising for the hurt and harm he caused: https://thebuddhistcentre.com/news/statement-urgyen-sangharakshita. In 2017–2019, the Adhisthana Kula, seven senior Order members, conducted an internal investigation with their final report published in 2020: https://alaya.thebuddhistcentre.com/index.php/s/64UhJHqoZWB7iLK#pdfviewer.

[21] The Adhisthana Kula state that this forms 'no part of Triratna teaching today'. Triratna's current refutation of these teachings can be read at https://thebuddhistcentre.com/controversy/.

effluences are seen as particularly polluting (Douglas 1966); many religious and cultural traditions worldwide maintain ritual practices around menstruation and childbirth. Women are frequently held responsible for maintaining not only their own embodied, sexual purity but through this, men's too. These ideas are illustrated by the purity culture of 1990s and 2000s Evangelicalism which promoted literature, conferences, and material cultures such as purity rings and pledges committing to abstinence until marriage (Fahs 2010; Moslener 2015; Allison 2021; Blyth 2021; Thwaites 2022). But this culture had older roots, such as in practices of older evangelical movements, as well as in wider society.[22] These practices are harmful in numerous ways as women in particular experience pressure to take responsibility for maintaining the sexual purity of the group; they are disciplined to have a preoccupation with maintaining their appearance and mannerisms, their very embodied being, to protect the purity of men. They must not wear revealing clothing or behave in any manner that could be considered flirtatious in case they tempt men into desiring sex. In this way, their intimate lives are regulated, and they are blamed and sometimes publicly humiliated for transgressions, a blame which is often then internalised.

Purification practices, and their role in abuse, can also be linked to teachings and practices around health and healing. Healing is interconnected with religion in numerous ways, not least because both are concerned with one's body, one's place in the world, one's self-development and one's salvation.[23] Leaving aside the issue of potential child abuse linked to the withholding of allopathic medicine, there are other ways in which a religious movement's health practices could enable abuse.

Abuse by healers and healthcare practitioners occurs across religious, cultural and secular contexts. Rutter included sex between doctors and patients as an example of sex in the 'forbidden zone', that is, a relationship of unequal power dynamics and hence an abuse of trust, but religion can add an additional layer of complexity (1989: 11). A religious healer can use the weight of religious authority, backed by a legacy of teachings, texts and practices, to pressure or coerce a follower into a sexual act or relationship. Healing practices can legitimise the context for abuse and/or they can be part of a grooming process, a precursor to abuse, particularly when they involve touch, such as massage. A number of reviews into abuse in Christian churches have highlighted massage as a harmful practice perpetrated in a coercive and controlling context, such as Jonathan Fletcher at Emmanuel Church Wimbledon and Mike

---

[22] Such as the 'civilizing process' described by Elias (1939), and in Victorian 'cultures of domesticity' (Welter 1966).

[23] Broadly understood, as in Beck and Beck-Gernsheim's concept of the modern 'health project' as a 'secular expectation of salvation' (2002: 141).

Pilavachi of Soul Survivor.[24] Peluso et al. (2020) have outlined the potential clash between expectations and experience when women attend South American ayahuasca healing rituals. They suggest that women are vulnerable to abuse because they are unfamiliar with the levels of nudity and touch expected and they give too much weight to the authority of the religious leader. But these points are equally applicable to other religious healing contexts. In movements in which there are already blurred boundaries around life and interpersonal relationships, and when there is a ritualised health technique at the centre, women can be particularly vulnerable to abuse. This vulnerability can be exacerbated through the lack of regulation and oversight of alternative health practices, in particular when movements also have a degree of social isolation and a claim to unique legitimacy.

## Punishment, Dissent and Disfellowshipping

Individual and group purity are inherently linked: a movement can only remain pure, and its unique legitimacy maintained, if all members are pure, that is, in alignment with the movement's teachings, practices and embodied norms. Some movements have developed specific practices around punishments for transgressions or dissent including disfellowshipping and shunning. Teachings and practices around punishments and associated mechanisms of excluding members are a further cluster of factors which can contribute to experiences of abuse. They can also prevent disclosures of abuse and/or increase the likelihood of a negative response to disclosure. Of course, punishing individuals who break the rules of an organisation is not unique to religious movements. What is unique are the perceived spiritual consequences of disobedience and the use of religious teachings – such as teachings on the importance of unity and forgiveness in Christian contexts – to legitimise punishment or to prevent people from speaking out about harmful elements. These factors can intersect with a movement's isolation and/or claims to unique legitimacy which can then entail a propensity for internal investigations of abuse claims. Accountability might be seen as due only to God, or to the leader of the movement, rather than to any form of external authority. However, internal investigations may prioritise the reputation of the organisation over reparation for survivors (IICSA 2021).

Some NRMs have practised the punishment of adult members who are believed to have transgressed rules or expressed dissent.[25] At the extreme end

---

[24] https://walkingwith.s3-eu-west-1.amazonaws.com/Final+Report+of+ECW+Review_March+2021.pdf and www.churchofengland.org/media-and-news/press-releases/concerns-substantiated-mike-pilavachi-investigation.

[25] Leaving aside here corporal punishment of children as a parallel although slightly different issue.

of the scale are movements which advocate physical punishment or threats of physical violence to keep members in line and dissuade them from leaving and/or speaking out against the movement. This was arguably most formalised in Jonestown where groups meetings, known as Peoples Rallies, discussed and dispensed punishments including beatings, the use of sedative drugs and confinement in small spaces (Wessinger 2000: 43). Group members themselves were integral to the dispensing of punishments, highlighting the horizontal group pressures and norms that had developed. This was alongside self-policing mechanisms, encouraged through the practice of public confession of sin and transgressions, as also occurs in Christian discipling practices. Moore describes the practice of 'corrective fellowship' in the early days of Peoples Temple in which members admitted to such transgressions as discourtesy to an elder, alcohol or drug use and petty crime. Over time, she writes, this practice evolved into 'catharsis' meetings which 'required public confession and communal punishment for transgressions against the community and its members' (2009: 32–3). This was a means of dispensing punishment and hence improving behaviour without resorting to external oversight (Moore 2012).

In other cases, however, it has been the inner circle who have been the primary target of physical violence perpetrated directly by the religious leader. Sogyal Rinpoche, leader of the Buddhist organisation Rigpa International, physically abused and publicly humiliated senior members who questioned his teachings, according to the eight former and current Rigpa students who wrote an open letter outlining their abuse at the hands of Sogyal Rinpoche in 2017.[26] This letter claims abuses were justified as 'crazy wisdom' teachings with the onus on students to accept and interpret beatings as spiritual teachings perpetrated with compassion.[27] As former nun and personal assistant to Sogyal, Damcho Dyson, has written: 'when Sogyal first "corrected" me, by striking me across the top of my head with a wooden back scratcher, I took this as a blessing' (Dyson and Newland 2019: n.p.). She emphasises the difficulties of recognising physical violence as abuse when it is seemingly legitimised by religious authority. Rigpa commissioned an independent investigation into the allegations and in 2018, Karen Baxter of Lewis Silkin LLP, published her report in which she concluded that some members of the inner circle were abused by Sogyal and

---

[26] Available at www.lionsroar.com/wp-content/uploads/2017/07/Letter-to-Sogyal-Lakar-14-06-2017-.pdf.

[27] The story of Marpa, who beat his disciple Milarepa, founders of the Kagyu lineage of Tibetan Buddhism, is often cited as a master of 'crazy wisdom' who uses 'unconventional actions to awaken a student' (Newland 2019 – https://beyondthetemple.com/does-tibetan-buddhism-condone-abuse/).

that senior teachers within the movement were aware of some of these abuses but did not address them.

Physical violence, an explicit form of harm and abuse, is not the only form of physical chastisement practised in religious movements. In Jonestown physical labour was also used as a form of punishment. Punishment for 'minor infractions' such as stealing food or using racist or sexist language, included 'such onerous chores as cleaning latrines, clearing fields after a harvest, and draining ditches of stagnant water'.[28] Other movements have promoted manual labour as both punishment and spiritual practice, sometimes drawing on monastic traditions of labour as spiritual discipline. Scientology's Rehabilitation Project Force (RPF) for instance provides a 'second chance' for Sea Org members who have 'failed to fulfil their ecclesiastical responsibilities'.[29] The movement's own literature describes this as 'a religious retreat in the form of a cloister focusing on intensive spiritual introspection and study and balanced by some form of physical labor'.[30] Furthermore, it is voluntarily undertaken, although usually after it is recommended by a 'Committee of Evidence', an internal investigation by peers (Pentikäinen et al. 2002). However, critics such as Kent (1997) have emphasised the pressures to attend when the other option is expulsion from the Sea Org. The Family International's Victor Program of the 1980s and 1990s had similar aims and practices. Directed at difficult teenagers, this programme combined 'a strict discipline of manual work and "word" study', with discipline that included 'extended periods of silence or isolation, as well as corporal punishment' (van Eck Duymaer van Twist 2015: 51). In one instance at least, at the Victor Camp in Macao, discipline also included the practice of exorcism (van Eck Duymaer van Twist 2015: 52–3). These punishment programmes hence combine different forms of harmful practices, including relocation, confinement and isolation from family and other forms of support. Manual labour as simultaneous punishment and spiritual practice could be an unhealthy blurring of boundaries, if combined with other factors such as verbal or physical abuse for transgressions.

Punishment does not have to be physical to move into the realm of abuse and harmful practices. Sogyal Rinpoche and Jim Jones both used tactics of humiliation. Abbott and Moore detail how Jones insisted that one woman strip to her underwear and jump into a swimming pool to 'teach her not to eat so much', and that another undress completely in front of a Planning Committee and listen to

---

[28] https://jonestown.sdsu.edu/?page_id=35333.
[29] www.scientologynews.org/faq/what-is-the-rehabilitation-project-force.html. This page makes clear that the rehabilitation programme is only applicable to Sea Org members – the 'religious order' of Scientology – not to rank and file members.
[30] www.scientologynews.org/faq/what-is-the-rehabilitation-project-force.html.

their criticisms of her body as punishment for an unknown offence (2020: n.p.). Keith Raniere, leader of the human potential organisation NXIVM, who was convicted in June 2019 of racketeering and sex trafficking, among other charges, encouraged female followers to send him sexually explicit photographs. He used these images to blackmail followers, alongside other coercive techniques including restricted diets, in order to maintain their participation in the inner circle of the movement (Helmore 2019).

These practices of bodily humiliation and blackmail are at one end of a scale; at the other end, participants more often maintain the rules and boundaries of their religious movements through their own convictions as well as peer group pressures to conform to norms and expectations. It is these that are at play in disciplining groups, alongside doctrines of unity and forgiveness. Although discipline and punishment were central concepts in the disciplining practices of, for example, the JFC and the ICOC, there is little information about what punishment in these groups actually entailed. However, survivor material (such as from the Jesus Fellowship Survivors Association and the ICOC lawsuits) makes clear that members believed there would be spiritual consequences for disobedience, including a generalised fear of falling from God's favour and being outside the fold of the community. All of these forms of punishment, from physical violence to manual labour to humiliation, blackmail and more, enforce conformity and inhibit dissent and criticism within movements. Those who have been subject to such punishment may be ostracised, isolated and further silenced within their movement (IICSA 2021). Punishment may also create pressures to remain in a movement, as fear of spiritual threats for oneself or one's loved ones, is an inhibiting factor.

Some new Christian movements do make their punishment practices clear. Some have developed systems which culminate in excluding, disfellowshipping and shunning members who have sinned and who show no remorse or repentance.[31] (It should be noted that Jehovah's Witnesses stopped using the terms disfellowshipping and shunning in 2024 [Chu and Peltonen 2024]). This is an explicit means of maintaining the purity of a movement as individuals perceived as problematic and impure are removed in order that they do not taint fellow members and 'contaminate' the organisation.[32] Jehovah's Witnesses are the most-cited Christian movement with this practice (Gutgsell 2017; Ransom

---

[31] While exclusion is a general term to indicate removing or keeping one apart from something, disfellowshipping has a more specific definition in Christian groups, such as Jehovah's Witnesses, where it is a form of discipline in which an unrepentant sinner is removed from the congregation. Shunning is the subsequent act in which remaining members having little or no social interaction with the disfellowshipped individual.

[32] https://wol.jw.org/en/wol/d/r1/lp-e/1995526?q=loving+provision&p=doc.

2022; Grendele et al. 2023) but it is also practised by the Plymouth Brethren Christian Church (PBCC) (Aebi-Mytton 2018; Doherty and Knowles 2021), the Christadelphians (Wilson 1961) and numerous house church movements, as well as in other religious traditions such as Haredi Jewish groups (IICSA 2021) and some Muslim groups (Bapir-Tardy 2016). Within these movements, these practices are a form of congregational discipline, as the onus is on community members to police one another's behaviour, with ongoing sinful behaviour reported to elders or other leaders within the movements.

Survivors and critics of these various groups have described shunning and disfellowshipping as abusive or harmful practices (Royal Commission into Institutional Responses to Child Sexual Abuse 2016; Gutgsell 2017; Aebi-Mytton 2018; Ransom 2022; Grendele et al. 2023). They argue that those who are shunned can experience emotional harm, trauma and other forms of diminished mental health (Ransom et al. 2021). They can be isolated and ostracised from their family, their friends and their place of work. They might fear that they are subject to damnation and outside of God's favour. Jehovah's Witnesses, for example, argue that this is the point, that this should encourage an individual into repentance and reinstatement within the movement – it is a 'painful correction' for one's 'own good'.[33] In August 2024, the Jehovah's Witnesses softened their language on this, removing the term 'judicial' from the committee of three elders who investigate claims of misconduct in order to ascertain whether a sin has been committed and whether the alleged perpetrator is repentant. Their literature now stresses that elders must be 'mild, gentle and kind' in their engagement with the removed individual, and that other Witnesses can greet the individual in the Kingdom Hall – previously even greetings were forbidden (Chu and Peltonen 2024; Watchtower Online Library 2024). However, historically, two-thirds of disfellowshipped Witnesses have not returned to the movement (Chryssides 2022: 40), suggesting that the practice might not achieve its desired effect of having removed members return (with the other desired effect being maintaining the purity of the congregation).

Former Jehovah's Witnesses in different countries have brought legal cases against the organisation to challenge their shunning, but without success. The first such challenge was brought by Janice Paul in Washington state in 1987, but the court did not uphold her claim 'regarding the Society's policy as a matter of religious freedom' (Chryssides 2022: 158; see also Introvigne 2021b: 62). This has been the common ruling in subsequent cases. Two court cases which initially ruled in favour of disfellowshipped members (Ghent, Belgium 2021 and Norway 2022) were overturned at appeal (Introvigne 2022b, 2023).

---

[33] www.jw.org/en/library/magazines/w20150415/disfellowshipping-a-loving-provision/.

Polarised views of shunning and disfellowshipping practices are unlikely to disappear. Survivors and critics suggest that shunning is an abusive practice; religious movements and their supporters, including NRM scholars who focus on issues of religious freedom, argue that it is within their religious freedom to practise the removal of members who commit offences. This is a non-negotiable practice which seems unlikely to be relinquished, and it is within a movement's religious freedom to engage in this practice, although survivors' lived experience of this as a harmful practice should be recognised. Shunning and ostracism are forms of punishment motivated by maintaining the purity of a religious movement which can contribute to difficulties in expressing dissent from within and with leaving a movement.

In this section, I have outlined four clusters of factors which can enable abuse in religious movements: social isolation and unique legitimacy; authority structures, including charismatic leadership; teachings on gender and sex; and punishment practices. These factors are not unique to NRMs. However, the structure and culture of NRMs can enable the intensification of some of these factors. In the next section, I analyse the abuses that occurred in the Jesus Fellowship Church using these factors. I argue that the structure of the movement – including its internal authority structures and its relationship with external society – and its culture of beliefs and practices created a harmful environment for some members. I show that the micro-regulation of members' lives, justified with religious teachings around discipleship and complementarian theology, contributed to the perpetration and concealment of abuse.

## 3 'A Holy Segregation Between the Sexes': The Jesus Fellowship Church

The JFC was an evangelical and charismatic movement founded in Northampton (UK) in the late 1960s, and which closed in 2019, partly in acknowledgement of the abuses that had taken place. The JFC is a pertinent case study to illustrate the ways in which structural and cultural factors intertwine to create abusive situations. The raison d'être of the Church – to create a community in which all things were shared in common, where differences between members were eliminated, and members' embodied lifestyle was an expression of their faith – entailed that cultural and structural factors were inextricably connected. The structure of the movement, including leadership hierarchies, discipling practices, family and gender relations, and relationships with wider society, were all based on interpretations of the Bible and created particular cultures within the movement. Members who lived communally disciplined their bodies, including their dress and appearance, their diet, their sexual practices, and their work and free time, to embody and demonstrate their Christian identity. The disciplining of bodies is a central way in which people live their religion and through which religious worlds are made (Hall 1997; Orsi 2004; McGuire 2008; Mellor and Shilling 2010). This is, of course, not by any means necessarily an abusive practice. However, as Orsi makes clear, there are also shadow sides and problematic elements because religion as lived can include 'intimate cruelties', 'abuses of power' and 'impulses to destroy and dominate' (2019: n.p.). Disciplining bodies, including those of children, can involve varying levels of discomfort, pain, suffering or harm, sometimes welcomed by an individual, sometimes not, and sometimes tolerated at the time but later recognised as harmful and abusive. There are varying degrees of agency within embodied religious disciplines and, in patriarchal religious traditions like the JFC, women and children have less agency than men. Abiding by a religious community's culture and norms involves operations of power which have different effects on different bodies.

The forms of abuse experienced in the JFC were varied and were experienced not only by some women but also by some children and by some men in the community.[34] Seven members or volunteers of the JFC have been convicted for sexual assault on other members, the majority of them minors. In Operation Lifeboat (2015), the police received over 200 claims of historical or non-recent abuse, including sexual, physical and emotional abuse, but the majority were not prosecutable as they were third-party reports and/or the victims were not traceable or were not supportive of police action.[35] The redress scheme, managed by the Trustees of the Jesus Fellowship Community Trust, hence includes both an Individual Redress Payment Scheme for those who experienced sexual, physical or emotional abuse in the JFC, as well as a Community Adverse Experience Scheme for those who witnessed the abuse of others and/or experienced other forms of harm, such as having relationships and access to the outside world controlled.[36] Such adverse experiences fit into Oakley's definition of spiritual abuse as 'a form of emotional and psychological abuse ... characterized by a systematic pattern of coercive and controlling behaviour in a religious context' (2018: n.p.). The adverse

---

[34] It is important to note that not all members experienced abuse. Some members were deeply saddened by the demise of the JFC, which embodied their ideal of Christian life, and have moved to other communal-living Christian communities.

[35] IICSA witness statement of Alastair White of Operation Lifeboat: https://webarchive.nationalarchives.gov.uk/ukgwa/20221215033512/https://www.iicsa.org.uk/key-documents/19139/view/NNP000028.pdf.

[36] Full list of experiences at https://jesus.org.uk/apply/community-adverse-experience/. Although it is not made explicit, it seems likely that this is drawing to some extent on the well-recognised psychological term 'adverse childhood experiences' (www.cdc.gov/violenceprevention/aces/about.html).

experiences were the result of coercive and controlling relationships in which religious doctrines, figures of religious authority and threats of damnation contributed to experiences of harm. The JFCT November 2021 Closure Statement outlines what it considers the 'systemic failings' of the Church, and I draw on this document throughout.

## Overview of the JFC

The JFC described itself as an evangelical, charismatic, and reformed Christian Church. Its founder, Noel Stanton (1926–2009), had been a lay minister at Bugbrooke Baptist Church, Northamptonshire, since 1957. Stanton and the young members of the Baptist church participated in the charismatic renewal movement that was gaining momentum in the United Kingdom at the time, reading relevant literature, attending events at other churches, and experiencing being filled with the Holy Spirit (Cooper and Farrant 1997; Barker 2020). Stanton reportedly felt called to establish a community based on the early Christian Church and in 1969 the JFC was formally established. The JFC sought to be a church open to all, including the most disadvantaged in society, evangelising to those whom other churches did not reach and eradicating 'social and racial divisions' within its communities (JFCT 2021: 5). Its aim was to demonstrate 'a living, rather than religious, Christianity' (JFCT 2021: 4). Over time, a number of associated organisations furthered this aim.

In 1974, members collectively purchased a former Anglican rectory, New Creation Hall, in Bugbrooke, and began the New Creation Christian Community for members who wanted to live communally. More properties were purchased throughout the 1970s and 1980s. The movement spread to other towns and cities, but Northampton remained its heart. Not all members lived communally; different levels of membership permitted different levels of engagement. Style Three Covenant Members were those who had made the Sevenfold Covenant Commitment and had chosen to live communally in the New Creation Christian Community. This was around 20 to 25 per cent of the membership at any one time. For instance, at the height of the movement's membership in the mid-2000s, the JFC had approximately 3,500 members, around 600 of whom lived in about 70 houses, each housing up to 40 people (Kay 2007: 157). By the time the Church closed in 2019, membership included around 1000 people, about 200 of whom were still living communally (Barker 2020: 103). Some 250 members of the New Creation Community had also worked in one of the JFC's affiliated 'kingdom businesses', which included a farm in Northampton, a building supplies shop, a building, heating and plumbing company, and a number of shops.[37] Members who lived and worked communally were more likely to experience the intertwined structural and cultural factors outlined in this section; to apply for the reparations available in the Community Adverse Experience Scheme the individual must have lived in the community for three months. Hence this section is predominantly concerned with the New Creation Christian Community.

In the early 2000s, outreach to, and support for, the disadvantaged became more formalised with the establishment of seven Jesus Centres. Housed in large public buildings that had been purchased by the Church, including a cinema in Northampton, these centres were one-stop shops, offering spiritual, social and practical support, serving subsidised food, providing showers and laundry facilities, running classes in English and IT as well as creative arts, citizenship and more.[38] The centres were well respected and were recommended by police and social services. As Orsi (2004, 2019) and Lynch (2015, 2022) have noted, the good works of Christian communities are sometimes enmeshed in a complex relationship with the shadow side, so that while power structures and doctrines can be utilised to embody a more fair and just society, they can simultaneously facilitate the abuse of some individuals.

The Trustees of the JFCT came to recognise this conflict between good works and abuse. In 2013, the five leaders of the JFC (the Apostolic Group) invited members and former members to provide information about their experiences of the Church, including abusive and harmful practices.[39] They received 133 disclosures of non-recent cases of abuse, mostly third-party reports. These disclosures were passed to Northamptonshire Police who, in 2015, opened a six-month investigation (Operation Lifeboat) to investigate these and additional disclosures. They investigated 214 referrals, and seven arrests were made. This resulted in six convictions for sexual and indecent assaults. However, 2013 was not the first time that the issue of abuse and harm was raised in the JFC. Critical information about the JFC had been circulating since at least the mid-1980s when its relationship with other Christian organisations was strained. It was expelled from the Baptist Union, asked to resign from the Evangelical Alliance

---

[37] 'So called because of the vision of "taking" money from the world and channelling it into the kingdom of God'. The kingdom businesses were considered a spiritual ministry, 'offering brotherhood, discipleship and in some cases rehabilitation to those who work for them'. https://web.archive.org/web/20120311121122/http://www.newcreation.org.uk/nccc/articles_fat cats.shtml.

[38] https://web.archive.org/web/20150330210005/http://jesuscentre.org.uk/about-london-jesus-centre.

[39] According to Barker (2022: 24) this was because the Church became aware that it would need to deal with historical and non-recent abuse cases as had other churches, not least the Catholics and Anglicans. The advice to ascertain the scale of the problem was given by the Church's legal and insurance advisors.

in 1986, and in 1989 was criticised by the Church of England Archdeacon of Northampton.[40]

It was arguably in the 2010s, however, that issues of child protection came prominently to the fore. In 2010, a former JFC volunteer, James Gardner, was convicted for sexually abusing three boys living in community in the 1990s. Gardner had previous convictions for child abuse but no criminal background checks were carried out before he was permitted to volunteer as a gardener at the community house in Coventry. Prosecuting judge, Charles Wide QC, stated that children would continue to be at risk of abuse unless the JFC updated its child protection systems.[41] Following this case, the JFC worked with the Churches' Child Protection Advisory Service (CCPAS now called Thirtyone:eight) to implement child protection policies. The JFC commissioned CCPAS to undertake a full safeguarding audit in 2015 and the two organisations implemented a service agreement to ensure that safeguarding was fully embedded.[42]

In 2017, the JFC commissioned a conflict management organisation to investigate the extent to which the five leaders (the Apostolic Group) were complicit in abuse through their 'failure to report abuse, interference with witnesses and mishandling of disclosures' (JFCT 2021: 3). The report is not publicly available but BBC analysis of a leaked copy states that the report concludes that the leaders 'must take responsibility for their inaction'.[43] The five leaders stood down, to be replaced by a JFC National Leadership Team, and it was this team who in 2019 advised remaining members to vote for revoking the Church's Constitution, as its problems were insurmountable. Northamptonshire Police's Operation Lifeboat Two, which investigated the concealment of abuse, concluded in 2020 with no prosecutions: the five leaders were questioned under caution but there was insufficient evidence to pursue criminal proceedings.

The JFC Redress Scheme began in 2021 and included financial distribution to current members to enable them to move to new living arrangements as well as compensation in the Individual Redress Payment Scheme and supported grants and return of capital in the Community Adverse Experience Scheme. Both the individual and community schemes also included written apologies and acceptance of responsibility by the JFC. The JFCT published its final report in September 2024 (JFCT 2024).

---

[40] This was in an ITV programme, 'Jesus Army – Church or Cult', aired 15/06/1989, www.jesusarmywatch.org.uk/scrapbook/television.htm.
[41] www.northamptonchron.co.uk/news/local/judge_jesus_fellowship_s_children_at_risk_of_abuse_1_899038 (no longer available online but held in Inform's electronic archive).
[42] https://thirtyoneeight.org/news/statement-following-the-closure-of-jesus-fellowship/.
[43] www.bbc.co.uk/news/uk-england-northamptonshire-53450901.

## Organisation and Lifestyle as Expressions of Faith

In her analysis of how three NRMs (ISKCON, TFI, and the JFC) responded to child sex abuse, Barker argues that three variables need to be taken into account: 'the social structure, the prevailing culture and the individuals involved' (2022: 14). She broadly categorises abuse within ISKCON as resulting from structural factors, abuse within TFI as resulting from cultural factors, and individual paedophiles as of particular significance within the JFC. She also recognises that in the JFC, 'the structure and culture permitted and indirectly enabled' abuse (2022: 14). I argue that this is even more the case when considering adverse experiences rather than specific instances of child sex abuse: the role of individual abusers is perhaps secondary to the ways in which structural and cultural factors can create potentially abusive environments.

Barker outlines similarities between the movements in terms of the structural and cultural interactions which enabled abuse. These include communal living arrangements, boundaries separating them from non-members, educational arrangements, lack of value placed on the biological family and unconventional attitudes towards sex. She writes that 'Theological beliefs had inspired all three [movements] to live in socially isolated communities that drew sharp boundaries between themselves and the outside world' (2022: 28). The communal lifestyle was central in JFC theology. It is a structural factor underpinned by doctrine, creating a specific culture through embodied practices and additional rules and dictates. Kay (2004: 89) states that the practice of communal living, rather than any 'doctrinal innovation', marked the JFC as distinctive. Living in community was seen as a modern expression of the lifestyle of the early Christians described in the Acts of the Apostles (Acts 2:44-5; 4:32-5). Members who chose to live communally made a commitment to the Sevenfold Covenant which outlined the central principles of the community.[44] This was both a lifelong commitment ('My intention is that for all my earthly life I shall be a covenant member of this Church and a soldier in the modern Jesus army', JFC 2007: 5) and an embodied one ('I want to serve Him by committing my whole lifestyle to Him', JFC 2007: 5). As will be described throughout this section, members cultivated their lifestyles and disciplined their bodies as expressions of this commitment, following rules as to what to wear and eat, how to interact with the opposite sex, whether to have sexual relations and how to raise children. As expressions of their new identity, they were also

---

[44] The seven principles are: Staying True to the Faith; The Holy Church of Brotherhood; The Holy Lifestyle of a Servant; The Community Life of God's People; Suffering with Christ; Discipling, Accountability and Discipline; and The Vow of Covenant (JFC 2007: 5).

given virtue names such as Faithful, Forthright and Gentle, reflecting either their character or their aspiration.

The seven principles of the Covenant stressed loyalty to the JFC as the true expression of the Christian faith and to a lifestyle of servanthood and suffering: 'I will deny myself and take up my cross to follow Him' (JFC 2007: 5). This was both an ideal – emulating the life of Christ – and a reality, as members pooled their resources into a common purse arrangement and agreed to live 'a Spartan existence' and a 'simple lifestyle' with few personal possessions or comforts (Hunt 2003: 114). During the 1990s, the seven principles were bolstered by a list of Forty-Eight Precepts which were essentially a list of do-nots to encourage the 'holy lifestyle' within the homes.[45] These included not doing the following: watching TV, listening to secular music, reading secular books, attending sporting events, concerts or other forms of entertainment, holding parties, taking holidays, having hobbies or 'amusements' and more. Members were encouraged to live modestly and seriously, rejecting 'selfish and worldly attitudes and behaviour' (JFC 2007: 5). They were taught that 'God's covenant people are not to love the world, nor the things in the world' (JFC 2000: 14) but should rather, through their lifestyle, show God's love to the world.[46] This lifestyle included an acceptance of persecution: 'I accept that this will cause me, with my brothers and sisters, to be opposed and hated and I will be ready to suffer with Christ for the sake of His Church in this way' (JFC 2007: 5). While Christ's suffering is a central trope within Christianity, in the JFC a sense of both group and personal persecution was welcomed as evidence of the Church's unique expression of 'the truth', of its unequivocal beliefs, and the loyalty of its members to each other and to the greater cause.

JFC literature in the 1990s and 2000s stressed that members entered into this covenant of their own free will (JFC 2007: 5), yet the Closure Statement recognised that teachings on forgiveness, loyalty and commitment contributed to 'systemic failings' in the movement. It recognised that these teachings, among others, placed 'onerous expectations' on members, to the detriment of 'family life, health and faith' (2021: 7), and that there was 'a misplaced vigilance for disloyalty to the "cause", stifling individual freedom of choice and self-expression' (2021: 8). Various authors (Oakley and Kinmond 2016; Lynch 2022) and public inquiries (IICSA 2021) have outlined the ways in which

---

[45] It should be noted that the precepts were largely used in the 1990s and the movement ostensibly became less strict over time. However, the JFCT's Closure Statement recognises that 'In later years, whilst some of these precepts or rules no longer applied, the overall culture and behaviour of the church and community life continued to follow similar objectives' (2021: 5).

[46] This is a quotation from 1 John 2:15-16. The JFC used the Revised Standard Version (1952) of the Bible and all Bible quotes in this section are from the RSV.

a doctrine of forgiveness has contributed to Christian churches' inadequate responses to abuse, as victims may be forced to forgive perpetrators or are otherwise silenced, promoting censorship and conformity.

The JFC practised communal living as the preeminent means to embody a Christian lifestyle which marked them out as God's true disciples. The second principle suggests the unequivocal and exclusivist theology in the statement 'I see this Church as separated from the world to shine as light in darkness and to show that Jesus Christ is Lord' (JFC 2007: 5). The JFC considered itself a holy society and, as such, its boundaries had to be policed and maintained. Beckford noted that cultural practices to 'define the purity/impurity boundary' are more pronounced in NRMs which seek to create 'refuges', set apart from the 'world's evil or illusions' (1985: 85). The practices and principles of communal living in the JFC portrayed the outside world and its behaviours as wrong and to be avoided. JFC materials were clear that interaction with 'worldlies' (non-members) was for the purpose of proselytisation only: 'We mix with the people of the world only to befriend and win them for Christ' (JFC 1991). However, communal living as an embodiment of radical faith is partly reliant on an audience. It created a holy lifestyle but was also a demonstration of, in their own terms, 'compassion in action', as the most socially disadvantaged were offered a combination of Christian teachings, practical support and, sometimes, a place to stay and to work. This created a situation in which people suffering from issues including mental illness, addiction, and prior offending, could stay in homes with families with no vetting, or checks and balances. The very mission of the JFC then, to present the gospel to the most marginalised, impoverished, and vulnerable in society, while helping many simultaneously contributed to the creation of an environment susceptible to abuse.

To operate in society, any religious movement must have a certain degree of engagement. JFC businesses were partly reliant on outside customers; social outreach programmes, including the Jesus Centres, needed a clientele to support and proselytise, and other Christian organisations were interacted with at different times and in different ways. The JFC had established its own network of independent charismatic churches – the Multiply Christian Network – but had a strained relationship with the Evangelical Alliance.[47] It had re-joined in 1999 but resigned for the second time in 2018 when the Alliance suggested that the JFC should come under the oversight of a more established denomination to increase its accountability. The JFC chose not to follow this advice, further isolating itself from the wider evangelical community.

---

[47] www.eauk.org/. The EA is the largest Evangelical network (open to both churches and individuals) in the United Kingdom.

## Leadership Structure and Discipling

The doctrines of communal living were supported through the Church's leadership and discipling structures. Founder Noel Stanton was the movement's initial charismatic leader, but over time he became supported by an organised network of senior leaders, pastors and assistant pastors who formed a hierarchical structure, in a process of routinisation (Prophet 2016: 38). Leadership passed to a senior leader on Stanton's death in 2009, then to an Apostolic Group of a handful of men and then, following the conflict management investigation, to a leadership team. In accordance with 1 Timothy 2:12 ('I permit no woman to teach or to have authority over men'), every senior leader, pastor – originally called an elder – and assistant pastor was male. The implications of this will be unpacked in the discussion of gender below.

Stanton could be described as a charismatic leader as followers acceded him authority over all areas of their lives and, during his lifetime, he had unique authority within the movement. This enabled a situation in which Stanton was able to abuse followers. The Closure Statement states that there were twenty-two allegations of abuse against Stanton, including sexual, physical, financial and emotional abuse: 'The Trustees believe it is likely Noel Stanton was at times the instigator of, or was at other times involved in, the abuse of both children and adults' (2021: 11). His lack of accountability as a charismatic leader can be seen as an abuse-enabling factor. The Closure Statement recognises that Stanton was not accountable, even to the senior leaders, and that his 'domineering' leadership created a 'climate of fear' within the movement. Stanton's 'domineering' and 'threatening' style was adopted by other leaders, as the correct model of leadership, so that this style pervaded the movement – not only among the senior leaders but among the pastors and assistant pastors who were the shepherds or heads of the communal households.[48]

The leadership structure was intimately connected to the practice of discipling within the movement. Seeking to live as a modern expression of the Apostles described in Acts, the JFC – in common with the majority of the house church movement and many charismatic and evangelical groups – adopted a discipling structure in which members were assigned a shepherd or discipler who was considered more mature in the Christian faith and hence capable of providing guidance and support to newer Christians. This structure modelled a doctrine of authority and submission. Shepherds had spiritual

---

[48] It should be recognised that there was some independence and autonomy in the way that the households were run, with different leadership styles on a spectrum from more authoritarian to more democratic, creating different experiences and living conditions for members in different houses.

authority over their flock (JFC 2000: 34) and, because they had been appointed based on their recognised spiritual qualities, they were to be obeyed: 'Obey your leaders and submit to them; for they are keeping watch over your souls, as men who will have to give account' (JFC 2000: 36, quoting Hebrews 13:17). Oakley and Humphreys point out that the characteristics associated with spiritual abuse were first identified in 'heavy shepherding' house church movements (2019: 5). They write, 'A hallmark of leadership in these settings was the requirement of those who followed to be submissive, to be willing to share details of their lives and to consult the "shepherd" ahead of making significant decisions, including job and relationship choices' (2019: 5–6). While they do not suggest that shepherding is an abusive practice in and of itself, it could be an enabling factor if there are no checks and balances in place.[49] For instance, the JFC document *We Believe* (2000) states that leaders are also subject to discipline and should be publicly rebuked if they sin. Yet in reality, the Closure Statement suggests, leaders did not hold one another accountable and rebuking them had serious consequences for less senior members. Those who challenged the authority of Stanton or other leaders could be '"relegated", "heavily criticised", "characterised as rebellious" and "told they would be subject to the judgment of God"' (2021: 6). This, combined with the Sevenfold Covenant's focus on loyalty to the JFC, contributed to cultures of conformity and silence, and to the barriers on dissent and speaking out that were recognised by IICSA (2021).

In the JFC, as in other groups with discipling practices, authority to the leaders and disciplers is acceded not just in the spiritual sphere but in all aspects of life; indeed, for the Covenant members who lived communally there was no distinction between different spheres of life as one's very way of living and working was an expression of faith. For those in community, there was no distinction between the religious movement and employment and living arrangements, and hence between the different interpersonal relationships associated with each sphere: the pastor had authority in one's religious life but also in one's home life and, sometimes, in the workplace too. Work was seen as an expression of Christian faith and hence, former members report, there was little leisure time – one's time and financial commitments were inextricably entwined in the movement. There was little distinction between private and public spaces, including in the communal homes which could be open to visitors and temporary guests and where members, including teenagers, slept in same-sex dormitories if they were not married. Few members in community had a private space, or the time to be there, values which are preeminent in the wider secular culture

---

[49] Writing from a Christian perspective, Oakley and Humphreys recognise that obedience is a central biblical discourse. 'However, the Bible is also clear that leaders should treat those they lead well and not abuse the power they have (Matthew 23)' (2019: 55).

from which members distanced themselves. The JFC discouraged leisure time and self-improvement, including discouragement from developing skills not sanctioned by the Church, such as participating in fitness and sports or cultural outings to museums and concerts (JFC 1991). Although many adults – although not the children – had chosen this lifestyle as an expression of, in their own terms, 'radical' Christianity, the enmeshed life likely contributed to difficulties in leaving the community.

Heads of households were responsible for the micro-regulation of householders' lives. Some members had little agency in their day-to-day lives as decision-making lay in the hands of pastors. The Closure Statement recognises that this created a situation in which 'adults living in community houses became institutionalised. Their ability to make decisions in respect to their own lives was compromised, with choice and agency removed' (2021: 6). Personal decisions around what to wear or eat were removed as strict rules and guidelines surrounded these embodied practices; householders ate simple food together, much of which was from the JFC farm, while takeaways and eating out were forbidden under the Forty-Eight Precepts. Decisions around what individuals could purchase and how much money should be allotted to them were also made by the heads of households and were frequently 'dependent on factors such as position in the hierarchy, personal relationships and gender' (JFCT 2021: 6). Personal finances were micro-regulated and, in some households, receipts of purchases were collected to manage this process. This was not then an equal community of believers but a hierarchical structure in which one's access to resources was dependent on being in good standing and accepting the authority of one's spiritual elders.

Central to the theology of discipling is the practice of discipline. Point six of the Sevenfold Covenant Commitment, entitled 'Discipling, Accountability and Discipline', reinforces the point that discipling is not simply an organisational structure, nor a means of dispensing Christian advice and wisdom, but also a means of maintaining the purity of the movement's boundaries. Sin threatens the purity of the community and is controlled through discipline. Those in the discipling or shepherding group confess their sins and faults to one another: 'I will confess my faults to my brothers and sisters just as they will confess their faults to me. I understand that there must be full openness within the brotherhood and that all must be accountable to each other. I will aim to welcome correction humbly and to easily forgive and be forgiven' (JFC 2007: 5). Survivor testimonies discuss 'accountability' sessions in which members confessed sins, including of a sexual nature. The Jesus Fellowship Survivors Association (JFSA) (2020) has written that micro-regulation of behaviour came not only from leaders but from fellow members as the commitment to group loyalty entailed the policing of others.[50] This led to 'being shamed/punished resulting in loss of trust in relationships, hypervigilance, paranoia, isolation of the individual'.[51] The JFSA suggests that discipleship was the primary means of control within the movement, executed through threats of exclusion and hence of damnation. In the JFC context, micro-regulation was formalised with a theology of discipleship.

## Teachings on the Family, Gender and Sex

The JFC had a complex relationship with the family as both an ideology and an institution. Many Christian movements, old and new, value the family in their doctrines and as the basis for their movement's organisation. The Church of Jesus Christ of Latter-day Saints practices the sealing of the family unit for eternity in the Temple, while Jehovah's Witnesses stress the importance of teaching and worshipping as a family – families will remain together in paradise on earth, providing that all members are saved. New conservative Christian movements which have developed out of the house church movement, such as the International Churches of Christ (Jenkins 2005) or New Frontiers International (Aune 2006, 2008), see themselves as creating 'awesome families' (Jenkins 2005), in terms of biological families situated within the movement, as well as the movement as a whole, or discipling groups within it, being considered a substitute or spiritual family. It should be noted that abuse nevertheless occurs both within families and movements that hold these doctrines: the upholding of doctrines valuing the family does not equate to a lack of abuse in practice. Some scholars (e.g. Dobash and Dobash 1980) have described the ways in which traditional, patriarchal authority structures can enable abuse in any family, religious or not. Nason-Clark (2000, 2003) argues that religious families do not have more instances of abuse but rather that within religious families, authority structures might be justified by theology, adding an additional layer of complexity. The theological element creates challenges in both recognising and disclosing abuse, as Christian women experiencing domestic abuse might be more likely to stay in a marriage they consider sacred before God (Nason-Clark 2000, 2003; McPhillips and Page 2021). Scholars looking at

---

[50] An organisation formed in 2018 by former members of the JFC, including those who had been raised within it from childhood. The group had various aims, including to support one another, to lobby for an independent inquiry and to seek redress and recompense from the JFC for abuses suffered: https://jesusfellowshipsurvivors.org/. A representative from JFSA, Sally Hirst, gave a testimony to IICSA for the report "Child protection in religious organisations and settings investigation report" (2021), available at https://webarchive.nationalarchives.gov.uk/ukgwa/20221215011833/https://www.iicsa.org.uk/key-documents/19121/view/public-hearing-transcript-tuesday-19-may.pdf.

[51] https://jesusfellowshipsurvivors.org/redress-scheme-wish-list-produced-by-the-jfsa/.

the intersections of religion and domestic abuse have tended to focus on women, but doctrines of the sacredness of the family also have implications for the treatment of children.

### The Place of Children in the JFC

Like Christianity in general, the JFC encouraged members to consider one another as family, with the discipling structure replicating a patriarchal family structure. The male pastor and his wife who served as heads of households took on a parental role, with other adults in the household having ostensibly equal roles as brothers and sisters, the preferred terminology for members within the movement. Brothers were discipled by the pastor, sisters by the pastor's wife. All adults, however, had positions of authority over children. In contrast to some forms of contemporary styles of parenting and teaching, where children are considered autonomous beings, with authentic emotional lives deserving of dignity, agency, rights and opportunities for creative expression, some more conservative styles of parenting, whether religious or cultural, consider children to be subordinate and in need of a firm hand of guidance, authority and, sometimes, punishment.[52] Indeed, another new Christian movement, the Twelve Tribes, ascribes much of what it perceives to be the current moral decline of society to the rise of parents' leniency towards their children, particularly permissive parenting from the 1960s onwards (Harvey and Newcombe 2021). In opposition to the wider culture they, like the JFC, have created an internal culture which they see as an authentic expression of true Christianity, which includes the submission of children to adult authority and the use of physical discipline.

In both the Twelve Tribes and the JFC, children were at the bottom of the hierarchical structure, and subject to the discipline of any adults within the community including, at times, the use of physical punishment. The Closure Statement (2021: 9) recognises that 'Children were inappropriately and harshly disciplined by adults, including those who were not their parents. At times in JFC's history, this included corporal punishment ("rodding")'. Conservative Christian movements' practice of rodding, disciplining with a wooden rod (or hairbrush, wooden spoon, ruler etc.) is an interpretation of Proverbs 13:24 ('He who spares the rod hates his son, but he who loves him is diligent to discipline him') and 22.6 ('Train up a child in the way he should go: And when he is old, he will not depart from it'), among other passages. While this is a non-negotiable and

---

[52] This is of course an oversimplification but on the nuances of styles of parenting and the construction of childhood see Hardyment (1983), Cunningham (2006), Lee et al. (2014), Strhan (2019) and Nilsson (2024).

unequivocal practice within the Twelve Tribes, and communities in Europe have had children removed from their care because of this practice (Wright and Palmer 2015), corporal punishment within the JFC was not practised consistently throughout its history or across households. Nevertheless, it is a significant factor contributing to harm experienced by some children in the community.

Children within the community also experienced other forms of harm. Children were at the bottom of the hierarchy, in a place of submission due to their age, and yet the JFC made no accommodations for children in terms of their requirements to follow the precepts and abide by the organisation's rules and regulations. The relevant precept states, 'Our families accept that all our precepts apply to children in community as well as adults'. This means that precepts such as 'We attend all meetings in the Church programme, arriving punctually and staying until the end' were equally applicable to children. The Jesus Fellowship Survivors Association describes an environment in which children had to attend all church activities, sacrificing time for homework, leisure and sleep.[53] The Closure Statement reports that 'children were made to partake in onerous schedules of worship or serving community needs' (2021: 9). In line with the cultural environment that adults also followed, children within the movement had no special place or consideration and their education, self-development, and creativity were not prioritised.[54] Children did attend local schools, but the precepts forbade them from attending extra-curricular activities, including sports and competitive events, and friendships outside of the Church community were discouraged or even prohibited in some households. Secular education was not valued and attending university was not encouraged. The Closure Statement views a 'suspicion of education' as a shortcoming of the movement. This applies not only to education as a value in and of itself but also to the education system as part of the 'outside', and therefore impure and sinful, world. Hence while children attended school, they could not develop interpersonal relationships there. Attendance at school but with none of the additional human skills such as making friends, sharing lunch, celebrating birthdays and festivals, meant that JFC children sometimes became targets for bullying. The Closure Statement recognises that when children did report bullying to a parent or pastor within the Church, they were sometimes

---

[53] https://jesusfellowshipsurvivors.org/redress-scheme-wish-list-produced-by-the-jfsa/. See also the JFSA Information Sheet for Counsellors (2018).

[54] This is in contrast to some NRMs which have assigned a special status and mission to their second and third generations, such as the Unification Church's 'Blessed Children' and the Children of God's Junior End Time Teens (see Palmer and Hardman 1999; Van Eck Duymaer Van Twist 2015; Palmer 2016; Frisk et al. 2018; Nilsson 2024). However, young people within the JFC did make a public commitment to the movement at the age of 15 or 16 and then became part of the 'J-Gen', with their own meetings and missions.

encouraged to welcome the persecution as an expression of an authentic Christian life (2021: 10). In this way, bullying was not addressed either in children's experiences or, likely, in adults' experiences within the community. Both the JFC and the JFSA saw this attitude towards bullying and education as a contributing factor to the adverse experiences of children raised within the movement.

Despite its emphasis on the importance of family, the JFC devalued biological family relationships in a number of ways, including by discouraging continuing relationships with biological family who were not members of the JFC; by valuing the practice of celibacy over marriage and reproduction; and by separating family units in the community. In some new Christian movements, including the JFC, detachment from previous relationships is reinforced with doctrines of purity, sin and salvation. It is only the group's members who are on the path to salvation and the purity of the group must be maintained through the avoidance of contamination with the secular world. The Forty-Eight Precepts are a clear example of the discipline of an embodied lifestyle to maintain the purity of the group. The final precept states, 'We uphold the practice of our precepts when visiting friends and relatives' (JFC 1991), indicating that although there was not a complete separation from non-member relatives, the Christian lifestyle as a marker of difference was to be upheld.

In community households, the discipling structure took precedence over the structure of the biological family. In some households, when children reached teenage years, they were removed from the care of their parents and placed in the care of a shepherd, either in the same house or another house in the community. Teenage children joined the sex-segregated single adults in households, sharing dormitories and the oversight of a shepherd, also of the same sex. It was this shepherd, not the parents, who had primary authority over the child: both parents and children had diminished agency and control. The Closure Statement reads, 'Many children were removed from their parents' household or influence in their teenage years and put under the responsibility of "shepherds" or "caring brothers/sisters", at times against the wishes of parents' (2021: 9).[55] The JFSA suggests that children 'lost' their parents because adult

---

[55] It must also be recognised that some parents agreed to this and welcomed the oversight of their children by shepherds. NRMs throughout history have developed new forms and structures of childcare (see Palmer and Hardman 1999; Van Eck Duymaer Van Twist 2015; Palmer 2016; Frisk et al. 2018; Nilsson 2024). It has not been uncommon for parents and children to be separated, sometimes across continents, as parents have continued missionary work and children have been raised collectively (in, for example, the Children of God, ISKCON, Sahaja Yoga, Unification Church, to name but a few). In her analysis of child abuse, Barker (2022: 29) cites a CoG mother who admits that she would have sent her daughter to another location, even knowing she might experience sexual abuse there, because she believed strongly in the movement's wider mission.

members were too consumed by Church responsibilities to have time and energy for their children, consequently they did not know what was happening in their children's lives and children had no one to advocate for them. This environment enabled opportunistic abuse, as all adults had access to and a position of authority over children. The Jesus Fellowship Redress Scheme's Final Report states that one in six children within the community were sexually abused (2024: 4). The lack of training, oversight and accountability of pastors contributed to potentially harmful living conditions for children within the movement. The Final Report states that 'four in every ten are estimated to have had adverse experiences in community' (2024: 4). JFC's views on gender relations and the promotion of celibacy were also factors, influencing the lives of all in the community, but, arguably, those of women in particular.

## Gender Relations

The JFC placed foremost value on celibacy, yet in reality this was a minority practice, with many members in traditional family relationships. Two concurrent authority structures operated within the JFC: the organisation of the movement as a whole, governed by the discipling structure, and family structures in which wives submitted to the authority of their husbands, children to their parents and other adults. As Maddox (2013) has noted with regard to the Australian evangelical organisation, Hillsong, the two structural forms are interconnected, as male headship within the family lends legitimacy to wider hierarchical power structures within the Church. Within JFC, as in Hillsong, structural gender relations were patriarchal and heteronormative, in line with the ideals of complementarian theology characterised by ideas of male headship and female submission. Complementarian theology has been recognised as a contributing factor in instances of domestic abuse/intimate partner violence (Nason-Clark 2000, 2003; Oakley and Kinmond 2016) and as contributing to gendered violence against women in religious communities more generally (Blyth et al. 2018; McPhillips and Page 2021; Shorter 2021). Without using this term, or providing much detail, the Closure Statement nevertheless recognises 'attitudes to women' as one of the Church's systemic failings, contributing to the abuse and adverse experiences of some members.

Complementarian theology is found across many Christian denominations, as well as across other religious traditions and in non-religious contexts, but is arguably more prominent in evangelical, Pentecostal and charismatic house churches and denominations where it aligns with other conservative social and political norms. Complementarian theology is the idea that two sexes were created equal but different and that gender roles, which map entirely onto biological sex, must reflect this, creating different roles, responsibilities and opportunities for men and for women. Within the Christian context, key biblical texts include Genesis 1–3 which recounts the creation, including of Adam and Eve (especially 2:18, 'Then the Lord God said, "It is not good that the man should be alone; I will make him a helper fit for him"'); Ephesians 5 (such as 22-23, 'Wives, be subject to your husbands, as to the Lord. For the husband is the head of the wife as Christ is the head of the church, his body, and is himself its Saviour') and 1 Timothy (such as 2:12, 'I permit no woman to teach or to have authority over men'). These texts are read as presenting the creation of man and woman as having different but complementary bodies, with their subsequent roles and positions – with woman as the 'helper' of man and as secondary – as divinely ordained. Man and woman come together in marriage: monogamous, heterosexual marriage is the only permitted context for sexual relationships in this theology (see Afzal and Stiebert 2024: 12–28).

Religious studies literature has examined whether these ideals are actually lived out in conservative Christian marriages, with numerous scholars arguing that the ideal is always negotiated and women find many opportunities for equality within marriage (Brasher 1997; Griffith 1997; Gallagher 2003; Ingersoll 2003; Aune 2006). These authors have studied complementarian theology as a boundary marker, as an ideal which distinguishes Christian communities from wider society. More recently, some authors have noted that the ideal is not in fact very different from the expectations of gender relations in mainstream society (Maddox 2013; Shorter 2021). Hence, if it is not a successful boundary marker on its own, nor a lived reality in Christian marriages, what purpose does it serve, what is its role in the lives of contemporary Christians? Analysing the Sydney Anglican Diocese, Shorter argues that complementarian theology is a 'religio-political discourse' which 'constructs orthodoxy and both creates and limits gendered and religious identity' (2021: 218). Maddox argues that in Hillsong 'headship forms part of a discourse about authority and submission that encompasses pastors' authority over laity, the state's authority over citizens, and Christian authority over secular society' (2013: 9–10). These functions of complementarian theology – as defining gendered religious identity and as part of a wider doctrine of authority and submission – were circulating within the JFC. It provided a biblical basis for ideas of authority and submission more generally and, alongside other beliefs and practices, it served to distinguish the JFC from the wider society and as a marker of true Christianity. But it also governed individual interpersonal relationships and lived experiences between men and women in the community, and contributed, sometimes, to experiences of abuse or to adverse experiences in which women in the community were not valued as equal human beings. The centrality of gendered religious teachings in abuse experiences emphasises the need for a widening of the focus in NRM studies beyond physical violence to include interpersonal, gender-based and sexual violence.

It could be argued that JFC members living a communal lifestyle embodied the complementarian theology ideal to a greater extent than those in Christian organisations more networked into wider society, such as the Sydney Anglican Diocese. The JFC *We Believe* document makes clear that the theology does not just cover gender roles in the abstract or ideal but in their actual performance: 'Male and female are equal in new creation status, both being sons of God in Christ Jesus. In this present age however, they are to be different in role, appearance and dress' (2000: 36). JFC community rules governed how men and women should look, with dictates against unisex appearance, particularly with regard to clothing and hairstyles. Women should not wear trousers; men should not wear women's clothing or grow their hair long, 'for whoever does these things is an abomination to the Lord your God (Deuteronomy 22:5)' (JFC 2000: 37). This is a strong admonition to exemplify restricted gender roles and appearances.

Complementarian theology also governed the roles and opportunities that were available to women in the JFC. The Closure Statement declares 'There was an expectation that women would give up their aspirations and careers to serve the church and men, taking domestic roles in community houses, for example, or behind-the-scenes administrative duties. Women living in community were not expected to return to employment after having children' (2021: 8). Women in the JFC were confined to the domestic sphere and the tasks of day-to-day life, such as cooking and cleaning, fell to them. The JFSA notes that children were socialised into gender-segregated roles from an early age, with girls expected to help with domestic chores in the houses, and boys with more manual tasks such as gardening and farming (2018: 6). It should be noted that although these gender roles do not differ from those in the secular mainstream, especially historically, the JFSA suggests that it was their combination with the radical lifestyle of heavy time commitments and with doctrines of purity and segregation which enabled gender roles to be contributing factors in experiences of abuse.

## Purity and Segregation

The JFC's complementarian theology and its dictates around appearance are intertwined with concerns around maintaining sexual purity. Within the JFC, as in most Christian denominations, marriage was the only appropriate context for sexual relationships, and any form of sex outside of marriage, including (and especially) gay relationships, was prohibited. Relationships between the sexes were highly controlled: 'We maintain a holy segregation between the sexes and do not allow flirtation' (JFC 1991). The JFSA notes that these ideas had most impact on lived experiences in terms of dating and friendships (2018: 9). Friendships between the sexes were discouraged or actively prohibited, including those in childhood. When people reached an appropriate age, they could date through a 'supervised "relating process"' (JFC 2021: 10). This was to maintain not only purity between the sexes but the purity and boundaries of the movement as a whole, as marriage was confined within the community: 'We believe that a Christian ought only to marry another Christian. This is in order for the relationship to carry unity. We also encourage marriage within our church covenant to further this working relationship in God's will' (JFC 2000: 32). Marriage within the community would create less tension for the couple, it was suggested, but also for the movement itself, with the biblical discourse of unity being a central tenet explicated in the Sevenfold Covenant Commitment. Marriage within the community (i.e. endogamy) is common across many religious movements, old and new, as is seeking guidance on dating and relationships in shepherding churches. The JFCT has arguably recognised the problems with this more than many shepherding churches in its statement that 'The Trustees believe third parties interfered inappropriately with decisions that were matters of personal choice of individuals who may have wished to enter into a relationship or friendship with another person' (2021: 10).

Within Christian teachings of sex segregation and purity, responsibility for maintaining boundaries through embodied practice primarily lies with women. Ideas stemming from purity culture were paramount in the JFC. One survivor describes how she was banned from one of the community houses at the age of twelve, which she later found out was the elder's move to protect her from men. 'I was told, in the words of one elder, that men "couldn't cope with me". Those words have haunted me ever since. It meant I was to blame for the abuse I'd received. I must have been provocative. I must have caused it'.[56] The JFSA has cited the practice of 'Women shamed and blamed for "stumbling"/ tempting men just by being women' as an example of the discriminatory abuse that women in the community suffered.[57] As in many religious movements, and in wider secular society, women had to police their own actions in order to maintain both their sexual safety and the purity of the movement as a whole.

---

[56] www.premierchristianity.com/home/i-left-an-abusive-christian-community/3552.article.

[57] https://jesusfellowshipsurvivors.org/redress-scheme-wish-list-produced-by-the-jfsa/.

These ideas have a number of implications for women. They can make women uncertain or ashamed about their own bodies and the appropriateness of everyday interactions with the opposite sex (Thwaites 2022). They create a lived experience of a generalised fear of potential sexual violence and women's supposed complicity within this. Purity culture is also inherently connected with discourses of shame. As Pattison points out, shame is not a single phenomenon with a single definition but rather constitutes a 'family' of 'overlapping meanings' (2000: 3). He suggests that 'it is best situated within the metaphorical ecology of defilement, pollution and stain' (2000: 88). Douglas's (1966) theory of dirt and pollution arising from a transgression of boundaries allows for an interpretation of sexual intercourse as both a transgression of bodily boundaries and, when the body stands in for the community, of moral and social boundaries. Interpretations of sex as dirty and polluting encourages the internalisation of shame of sexual urges and of bodily functions. This was reinforced in the JFC with its encouragement for members to recount sexual sins to maintain the purity of the community and its valuing of celibacy, which suggested the potential for transcendence of embodied sins.

As in other purity cultures, there was a preoccupation with sexual sin more generally in the JFC. Sexual sins were shared within shepherding groups in order that appropriate punishments be meted out, including in 'accountability' sessions. One ex-member described this as confessing all of your faults and sins, including of a personal and intimate nature, to male elders. JFSA materials assert that the preoccupation with sexual sin, including masturbation, created a situation in which bodily processes and functions were considered dirty and polluting. The JFSA describe a practice of 'Unhealthy preaching – anything relating to desires/sex/needs/bodily functions demonised during sermons'.[58] Unlike a number of other evangelical churches, the JFC did not seem to celebrate or value sexual intercourse even within marriage. Sexual intercourse was for the purpose of procreation alone, sex itself was sinful, and celibacy was the preeminent value within JFC.

## *Teachings on Celibacy*

The JFC saw celibacy as a higher path than married life. Akin to the value placed on spiritual renunciates in other traditions and across history, celibacy was promoted as a means of increasing commitment to the Church and to God's work, without the distraction of a family. Quoting passages from 1 Corinthians 7, the *We Believe* booklet states, 'Celibacy is a more favourable gift than marriage because it frees people from the cares of married life. Celibates have

---

[58] https://jesusfellowshipsurvivors.org/redress-scheme-wish-list-produced-by-the-jfsa/.

undivided devotion to the Lord' (2000: 33). 'Undivided' was the name of the newsletter the JFC produced for its celibate members, with a subtitle from 1 Corinthians 7:35 – 'to secure your undivided attention for the Lord'. The rationale for celibacy was phrased in terms of the increased devotion and time celibate people can give, rather than in terms of the avoidance of pollution through sex. But the JFC's ambiguous relationship with sex, even within marriage, was enmeshed in this doctrine. In footage of a sermon from 1993, Noel Stanton encouraged his congregation to surrender their voices to the Lord, surrender their 'middle parts' to the Lord, 'especially the genitals', as 'an awful power of sin lurked there'.[59] Giving their 'genitals to Jesus' as he exhorts, that is, turning to a life of celibacy, could be a means of avoiding the potential of sexual sin.

Living a celibate life was seen by the JFC as another aspect of living the radical Christian lifestyle and as modelling the life of Jesus. It was another way in which members disciplined their bodies to follow a life which marked them out as true Christians. As McGuire writes, 'when a religious group contests the dominant society's meanings of gender, sexuality and other body-relevant aspects of the self, it must actively promote spiritual practices to reshape its members' bodily experience and expression' (2008: 173). The JFC's complementarian theology did not challenge dominant norms, but its practice of celibacy did. The bodily practices of sex, what the body does or, in the case of celibacy, does not do, is part of the everyday lived experience which maintained JFC's religious worldview.

Celibacy was a public practice in that members made a celibacy pledge to the community. It was not simply a personal, private decision that could be practised or relinquished, but was rather a communal pledge to a lifetime commitment (after a year's probationary period). Around 300 people made this pledge during the JFC's history, not only young people but also widows/ers, divorcees, single parents and LGBT members. The Closure Statement recognises that the value placed on celibacy may have led people to feel pressured into 'making a celibacy vow without adequate counselling, preparation or maturity' (2021: 10). The value placed on celibacy also devalued marriage, family life and the domestic sphere: that is, everything associated with the women of the community through their restricted gender roles. In this way, it served as a further means of relegating the status of women and children within the community, who were implicitly portrayed as a distraction on men's path to salvation. This can be considered a form of gendered discursive violence in its legitimisation of inequality.

---

[59] www.bbc.co.uk/news/av/uk-england-northamptonshire-53657504.

## Abuse in the JFC

This section has discussed the major structural and cultural factors of the JFC: its organisation and lifestyle as an expression of faith, and its interconnected teachings on the family, gender relations, and sex. The JFC theologically justified its practice of communal living with biblical texts, most notably Acts of the Apostles, and with additional internal documents, including the Sevenfold Covenant and, for a time, the Forty-Eight Precepts. These texts covered, and encouraged, teachings around servanthood, suffering and persecution, forgiveness, and exclusivist teachings, including a degree of separation from the world, all of which contributed to the harms experienced by some. Inherently connected to the communal living practice was the movement's leadership structure and practice of discipling, which was also biblically justified. This created a structure of authority and submission in which some men had positions of authority and were largely unaccountable to the wider membership. The formal organisational structure also provided more opportunities for more leaders to misuse power. Male leaders, as disciplers and shepherds, regulated the lives of householders, who experienced little agency over their personal lives, including dress, diet, finances and interpersonal relations. According to survivors, regulation through a theology of discipling was a primary means of control within the movement.

The movement's teachings about family and gender relations were an integral part of the structures of authority and submission. Complementarian theology is an authority structure which places men at the apex of an authority pyramid with women and children in positions of submission. In the JFC, these teachings were intensified by the break-up of family units once children reached their teens, the lack of value placed on children's education, autonomy, creativity and leisure time, and the preeminent value placed on celibacy. The valuing of celibacy, although only practised by a minority within the movement, suggested that children and married women were distractions to men's Christian lives.

I have concentrated on the ways in which structural and cultural factors intertwined to enable what the JFC itself has termed 'adverse experiences' for some of those who lived in community, and not simply on allegations or convictions of sexual abuse. JFC never justified such abuse. Rather, hierarchical authority structures and power relations created an environment in which abuse of different, intersecting forms was possible and disclosure was difficult. It was the ways in which the conflation of beliefs and practices came together in an embodied lifestyle that generated an abusive environment for some members.

## 4 Conclusion

The factors which facilitate abuse described in this Element are not only applicable to religious contexts. Abuse can occur in any context in which there are hierarchies of power, as the increasing public recognition of abuse in sports training, music and dance academies, universities, businesses and politics demonstrates. In each of these contexts, there are structural and cultural factors which interconnect to enable abuse to be perpetrated and concealed. There are factors unique to each organisation, but it is also possible to identify common, broad, structural and cultural factors. These include an organisation's engagement with wider society, other organisations and policies, such as safeguarding. It also includes the ability of people within the organisation to seek external advice and support. It includes the leadership structures and forms of authority held by those in charge, and the impact of this on those lower in the hierarchy, including whether they can maintain clear boundaries around different spheres, activities and people in their lives. Gender relations are also paramount – whether there is a gender bias in the organisation or, indeed, direct or indirect discrimination based on gender, race, class, age, sexual orientation and disability. Also important is the extent to which the organisation's beliefs, practices and procedures are taken as unequivocal and whether there are forms of punishment for transgressing these unequivocal procedures or pressures not to transgress or even question at all. These are the factors this Element has examined.

However, there are also certain aspects unique to religious contexts, brought about by the introduction of the metaphysical realm into the dynamic. To a believer, a religious leader, text or tradition can carry more authoritative weight than a leader, text or tradition in the non-religious contexts noted above; their authority extends to represent a metaphysical force – whether this be God, another deity or a conception of power, energy or enlightenment. This is the essence of Oakley's (2018) concept of spiritual abuse: abuse in a religious context not only incorporates religious elements into the abuse (the weaponisation of scripture, texts and traditions) but also affects the individual's religious life (their relationship with the metaphysical source and their understanding of their place in the world and, potentially, beyond this lifetime). In this, there is something unique about abuse in religious contexts. The metaphysical dimension adds an additional layer of authority, has an effect on the individual's metaphysical frame of reference and can contribute barriers to the movement's propensity to change and to eradicate harmful dynamics and practices.

The factors I have discussed throughout this Element are potentially applicable to all religious contexts and thus I have not suggested that there is anything unique about abuse in NRMs. However, what I do suggest is that these factors can be intensified in NRMs. Barker (2004) defined NRMs as being comprised of a first generation of converts. From this central characteristic further variables can be identified. These include the enthusiasm with which members adhere to the beliefs, practices and authority of the leader, on the one hand, and the leader's desire to keep the members separate from the world in order to maintain this enthusiasm and adherence, on the other. This can contribute to environments of totalism, high-demand or blurred boundaries to a greater extent than in religious movements which have less strict boundaries and commitments. And these environments can be – although are not always – conducive to the perpetration and concealment of abuse. In Barker's words, these characteristics could 'predispose' NRMs 'toward situations in which harm might ensue' (2002b: n.p.). However, another important variable identified by Barker, is NRMs' tendency for rapid change, especially as a second generation is born into the movement requiring greater engagement with outside society. The propensity for harmful environments lessens as the movement matures and defines itself less in opposition to the mainstream. There are also religious movements, old and new, in which an opposition to wider society is inherited through the generations (for example, Haredi Jewish communities). Pathways of potential change have not been a focus of this Element, however.

Studying abuse in the context of NRMs allows us to see examples at one end of a continuum. The case study of the Jesus Fellowship Church examined a small, tight-knit, relatively isolated movement with strong boundaries with wider society and strict hierarchies of power determined by gender, age and spiritual adeptness. Separation from wider society is an important risk factor, but it is not the only one, and the other factors discussed in this Element can be present in more mainstream movements, including major Christian denominations. However, analysing abuse at the more extreme end of the scale – in terms of social structure, size, unequivocal beliefs and commitment – can illuminate wider processes and factors applicable in other, broader contexts. NRM scholars such as Beckford (1985) have long argued that as small social experiments, which arise in opposition to and hence challenge the mainstream, NRMs can provide insights into how controversial issues arise and are managed across other areas of society. They are useful sites for analysing broader themes of controversy, including harm and abuse. I hope that the factors described in this Element, developed from NRM studies, will be useful in analysing abuse across a range of contexts, not only religious ones.

This work also suggests the importance of continuing to build bridges between NRM and cultic studies, as well as with those investigating abuse in other religious and non-religious contexts. I suggested that on a practical, day-to-day level of trying to help those whose lives have been impacted in some way by new religions, there is little difference in the approaches of research-oriented cult-watching groups such as Inform and cult awareness groups such as the International Cultic Studies Association. This is partly due to Barker's philosophy of dialogue (ICSA 2013; Ashcraft 2018). However, it would be naïve to think that differences do not remain in the fields, and that everyone is now in agreement in their analysis and practical advice.

There will always be some insurmountable differences and some individuals in both fields who do not engage with the other side. Anticipating critique of this Element from within NRM studies, some might argue that I have used negative, atypical examples to extrapolate to NRMs in general, giving a skewed and inaccurate picture. This is not my intention. The focus of this Element is on abuse rather than on NRMs in general, as it is part of a survivor-centred project. I have drawn on NRM research in order to present a theoretical model of structural and cultural factors which can enable abuse. I have not suggested that these factors characterise NRMs. Criticism from the cultic studies side might consider this Element a case of too little, too late. Cultic studies scholars might argue that they have long emphasised ex-member accounts of harm and abuse and that this has been neglected in NRM studies. This point has also been made by feminist NRM scholars who state that their critical analyses of gender roles were neglected or even silenced due to the prioritisation of issues of religious freedom, meaning-making and particular conceptualisations of violence (Jacobs 1991, 2007). It is necessary to learn from this oversight and I agree that NRM understandings of violence should be widened to include harm and abuse, interpersonal and sexual violence. In this widened focus, it is useful to engage with other disciplines, including sociological studies of domestic violence which have identified mechanisms of abuse, such as coercive control (Stark 2007) and gaslighting (Sweet 2019). Engaging with these disciplines is not the same as equating coercive control with discredited theories of brainwashing.

Issues of harm and abuse and the mechanisms of coercive control and gaslighting are increasingly coming to the fore in wider society and in disciplines beyond NRM/cultic studies and studies of domestic violence. The study of religion, across disciplines, now prioritises such issues as the circulation of power, social justice and inequalities, building on a number of 'cultural turns' (Lynch 2012). This comes from new attention to lived religion, embodiment, emotions and materiality, as well as moves to deconstruct the category of religion (McCutcheon 1997) and decolonialise its study (Nye 2019). There is a concurrent rise in activist scholarship, which affirms that it is no longer appropriate to simply describe the world as we find it for the sake of knowledge but rather there is a need and obligation to call out injustices and to make positive changes in the world. This has led to a greater commitment to collaborative research in which those with personal experience of the injustices in question are essential and equal partners at every level of the research. Related to these trends, there is increasing academic research and policy interest in what have been termed high-demand, high-control religious movements. This incorporates a broader field of vision than NRMs and is a movement away from the cult category to include branches of all mainstream religions in which people feel they have been harmfully controlled. This terminology prioritises people's subjective experiences and self-definitions across religious movements. It must be recognised that what one person experiences as high-demand, high-control might not be described as such by someone else in the same group. However, this framing at least considers behaviour rather than labelling particular types of religious movements as cults.

The unearthing and analysis of abuse across all religious movements looks set to continue and NRM studies must engage with these recent developments, highlighting what its long history can add to the debate. It is through engagement with other scholars, disciplines and theories that we might collectively come to understand the issue of abuse in religious and non-religious contexts. This Element aims to contribute to the endeavour of understanding abuse in religious contexts in order first to better identify and ultimately to better address it.

# References

Abbott, Catherine B. and Rebecca Moore (2020) 'Women's Roles in Peoples Temple and Jonestown'. *The Jonestown Project* website. https://jonestown.sdsu.edu/?page_id=102062 (accessed 14 February 2025).

Adhisthana Kula (2020) *Addressing Ethical Issues in Triratna: A Report on the Work of the Adhisthana Kula*. August 2020. Alaya: The Triratna Cloud. https://alaya.thebuddhistcentre.com/index.php/s/64UhJHqoZWB7iLK#pdfviewer (accessed 14 February 2025).

Aebi-Mytton, Jill (2018) 'A Narrative Exploration of the Lived Experience of Being Born, Raised in, and Leaving a Cultic Group: The Case of the Exclusive Brethren'. DPsych thesis Middlesex University/Metanoia Institute Psychology.

Afzal, Saima and Johanna Stiebert (2024) *Marriage, Bible, Violence: Intersections and Impacts*. London: Routledge Focus.

Allison, Emily Joy (2021) *#ChurchToo: How Purity Culture Upholds Abuse and How to Find Healing*. Minneapolis, MN: Broadleaf Books.

Ammerman, Nancy T. (1987) *Bible Believers: Fundamentalists in the Modern World*. New Brunswick, NJ: Rutgers University Press.

Anderson, Kristin L. (2009) 'Gendering Coercive Control'. *Violence against Women* 15(12): 1444–57.

Anthony, Dick (1990) 'Religious Movements and "Brainwashing" Litigation: Evaluating Key Testimony' in Thomas Robbins and Dick Anthony (eds.) *In Gods We Trust: New Patterns of Religious Pluralism in America*. New Brunswick, NJ: Transaction, pp. 295–341.

Ashcraft, William Michael (2018) *A Historical Introduction to the Study of New Religious Movements*. London: Routledge.

Aune, Kristin (2006) 'Marriage in a British Evangelical Congregation: Practicing Postfeminist Partnership?'. *The Sociological Review* 54(4): 638–57.

Aune, Kristin (2008) 'Evangelical Christianity and Women's Changing Lives'. *European Journal of Women's Studies* 15(3): 277–94.

Bapir-Tardy, Savin (2016) 'The Practice of Shunning and Its Consequences'. *Sedaa: Our Voices*. 11 November 2016. www.sedaa.org/2016/11/the-practice-of-shunning-and-its-consequences/#:~:text=All%20of%20the%20negative%20beliefs,a%20long%2Dterm%20psychological%20torture (accessed 14 February 2025).

Barker, Eileen (1984) *The Making of a Moonie: Brainwashing or Choice?* Oxford: Blackwell.

Barker, Eileen (1989) *New Religious Movements: A Practical Introduction.* London: HMSO.

Barker, Eileen (1993) 'Charismatization: The Social Production of "an Ethos Propitious to the Mobilization of Sentiments"' in Eileen Barker, James Beckford and Karel Dobbelaere (eds.) *Secularization, Rationalism and Sectarianism: Essays in Honour of Bryan R. Wilson.* Oxford: Clarendon Press, pp. 181–201.

Barker, Eileen (2002a) 'Watching for Violence: A Comparative Analysis of Five Cult-Watching Groups' in David G. Bromley and J. Gordon Melton (eds.) *Cults, Religion and Violence.* Cambridge: Cambridge University Press, pp. 123–48.

Barker, Eileen (2002b) 'Harm and New Religious Movements (NRMS): Some Notes on a Sociological Perspective'. *Cultic Studies Review* 2(1). https://articles1.icsahome.com/articles/harm-and-new-religious-movements–nrms–some-notes-on-a-sociological-perspective (accessed 14 February 2025).

Barker, Eileen (2004) 'What Are We Studying? A Sociological Case for Keeping the "Nova"'. *Nova Religio* 8(1): 88–102.

Barker, Eileen (2009) 'In God's Name: Practising Unconditional Love to the Death' in Madawi Al-Rasheed and Marat Shterin (eds.) *Dying for Faith: Religiously Motivated Violence in the Contemporary World.* London: I. B. Tauris, pp. 49–58.

Barker, Eileen (2011) 'Stepping Out of the Ivory Tower: A Sociological Engagement in "the Cult Wars"'. *Methodological Innovations Online* 6(1): 18–39.

Barker, Eileen (2014) 'The Not-So-New Religious Movements: Changes in "the Cult Scene" over the Past Forty Years'. *Temenos* 50(2): 235–56.

Barker, Eileen (2017) 'From Cult Wars to Constructive Cooperation – Well, Sometimes' in Eugene V. Gallagher (ed.) *'Cult Wars' in Historical Perspective: New and Minority Religions.* London: Routledge, pp. 9–22.

Barker, Eileen (2020) 'Denominationalization or Death? Comparing Processes of Change within the Jesus Fellowship Church and the Children of God aka the Family International' in Michael Stausberg, Carole M. Cusack and Stuart A. Wright (eds.) *The Demise of Religion: How Religions End, Die, or Dissipate.* London: Bloomsbury, pp. 99–118.

Barker, Eileen (2022) 'What Did They Do about It? A Sociological Perspective on Reactions to Child Sexual Abuse in Three New Religions' in Beth Singler and Eileen Barker (eds.) *Radical Transformations in Minority Religions.* London: Routledge, pp. 13–39.

# References

Barlow, Richard (2017) 'The Unification Movement: Past and Future' in Eugene V. Gallagher (ed.) *'Cult Wars' in Historical Perspective: New and Minority Religions*. London: Routledge, pp. 121–34.

Baxter, Karen (2018) 'Report to the Boards of Trustees Of: Rigpa Fellowship UK, and Rigpa Fellowship US'. Lewis Silkin LLP. https://static1.squarespace.com/static/580dbe87e6f2e16700cb79fe/t/5b8f7c1e1ae6cfb38491e668/1536130081917/Lewis+Silkin+report.pdf (accessed 14 February 2025).

Beck, Ulrich and Elisabeth Beck-Gernsheim (2002) *Individualization: Institutionalized Individualism and Its Social and Political Consequences*. London: Sage.

Becker, Howard (1932) 'Processes of Secularisation: An Ideal-Typical Analysis with Special Reference to Personality Change as Affected by Population Movement'. *Sociological Review* a24(3): 138–54.

Beckford, James (1985) *Cult Controversies: The Societal Response to the New Religious Movements*. London: Tavistock.

Bloom, Colin (2023) *Does Government 'Do God'?: An Independent Review into How Government Engages with Faith*. https://assets.publishing.service.gov.uk/government/uploads/system/uploads/attachment_data/file/1152684/The_Bloom_Review.pdf (accessed 14 February 2025).

Blyth, Caroline (2021) *Rape Culture, Purity Culture, and Coercive Control in Teen Girl Bibles*. London: Routledge.

Blyth, Caroline, Emily Colgan and Katie B. Edwards (eds.) (2018) *Rape Culture, Gender Violence and Religion: Biblical Perspectives*. Cham: Palgrave Macmillan.

Borecka, Natalia (2023) 'US Christian Group Accused of Covering Up Sexual Abuse of Minors'. *The Guardian*, 19 March. www.theguardian.com/us-news/2023/mar/19/international-churches-of-christ-lawsuits-alleged-sexual-abuse (accessed 14 February 2025).

Brasher, Brenda E. (1997) *Godly Women: Fundamentalism and Female Power*. New Brunswick, NJ: Rutgers University Press.

Bromley, David G. (ed.) (1998) *The Politics of Religious Apostasy: The Role of Apostates in the Transformation of Religious Movements*. Westport, CT: Praeger.

Bromley, David G. (2011) 'Deciphering the NRM-Violence Connection' in James R. Lewis (ed.) *Violence and New Religious Movements*. Oxford: Oxford University Press, pp. 15–31.

Bromley, David G. and J. Gordon Melton (eds.) (2002) *Cults, Religion and Violence*. Cambridge: Cambridge University Press.

Children of ISKCON v. ISKCON (2000) United States District Court, Northern District of Texas, Dallas Division.

Chryssides, George D. (2021) 'Charisma – Elusive or Explanatory? A Critical Examination of Leadership in New Religious Movements'. *Fieldwork in Religion* 16(1): 35–54.

Chryssides, George D. (2022) *Jehovah's Witnesses: A New Introduction*. London: Bloomsbury.

Chryssides, George D. (2024) 'A History of Anti-Cult Rhetoric' in Aled Thomas and Edward Graham-Hyde (eds.) *'Cult' Rhetoric in the 21st Century: Deconstructing the Study of New Religious Movements*. London: Bloomsbury, pp. 62–90.

Chryssides, George D. and Stephen E. Gregg (eds.) (2019) *The Insider/Outsider Debate: New Perspectives in the Study of Religion*. Sheffield: Equinox.

Chu, Jolene and Ollimatti Peltonen (2024) *Jehovah's Witnesses*. Cambridge: Cambridge University Press.

Cohen, Stanley (1972) *Folk Devils and Moral Panics*. London: MacGibbon and Kee.

Cooper, Simon and Mike Farrant (1997) *Fire in Our Hearts: Story of the Jesus Fellowship/Jesus Army*. Northampton: Jesus Fellowship Resources.

Cunningham, Hugh (2006) *The Invention of Childhood*. London: BBC Books.

Dawson, Lorne L. (2000) 'Religious Cults and Sex' in Clifton D. Bryant (ed.) *The Encyclopedia of Criminology and Criminal Behavior*. New York: Taylor & Francis, pp. 323–6.

Dawkins, Richard (2006) *The God Delusion*. London: Bantam Press.

Deslippe, Philip and Stacie Stukin (2020) 'Yogi Bhajan, Yoga Guru and Founder of 3HO, "More Likely than Not" Sexually Abused Followers, Says Report'. *Religion News Service*, 18 August. https://religionnews.com/2020/08/18/yogi-bhajan-yoga-guru-and-founder-of-3ho-more-likely-than-not-sexually-abused-followers-says-report/ (accessed 14 February 2025).

Dobash, R. Emerson and Russell Dobash (1980) *Violence against Wives: A Case against the Patriarchy*. London: Open Books.

Doherty, Bernard and Steve Knowles (2021) 'Plymouth Brethren Christian Church' in James Crossley and Alastair Lockhart (eds.) *Critical Dictionary of Apocalyptic and Millenarian Movements*. www.cdamm.org/articles/plymouth-brethren (accessed 14 February 2025).

Douglas, Mary (1966) *Purity and Danger: An Analysis of Concepts of Pollution and Taboo*. London: Routledge and Keegan Paul.

Dubrow-Marshall, Roderick P. (2024) 'The Recognition of Cults' in Aled Thomas and Edward Graham-Hyde (eds.) *'Cult' Rhetoric in the 21st Century: Deconstructing the Study of New Religious Movements*. London: Bloomsbury, pp. 150–74.

Dyson, Damcho and Tahlia Newland (2019) 'This Is Abuse'. *Tricycle*. 15 July 2019. https://tricycle.org/article/rigpa-abuse/ (accessed 14 February 2025).

Elias, Norbert (1939) *The Civilizing Process*. Oxford: Blackwell.

Fahs, Breanne (2010) 'Daddy's Little Girls: On the Perils of Chastity Clubs, Purity Balls and Ritualised Abstinence'. *Frontiers* 31(3): 116–42.

The Family Survival Trust (2022) *Controlling or Coercive Behaviour in the Wider Community: Proposal for New Legislation*. www.thefamilysurvival trust.org/_files/ugd/b17260_d84acbbb99cd4fd9875972186e15e048.pdf (accessed 14 February 2025).

Feuchtwang, Stephan (2008) 'Suggestions for a Redefinition of Charisma'. *Nova Religio* 12(2): 90–105.

Fletcher, Yehudis (2023) 'Religious Freedom Cannot Justify the Failure to Educate'. *The Times*, 2 March. www.thetimes.co.uk/article/yehudis-fletcher-religious-freedom-failure-educate-hasidic-jewish-schools-investigation-uk-xg5j30g8t (accessed 14 February 2025).

French, John and Bertram Raven (1959) 'The Bases of Social Power' in Dorwin Cartwright (ed.) *Studies in Social Power*. Ann Arbor: The University of Michigan Press, pp. 150–67.

Frisk, Liselotte, Peter Åkerbäck and Sanja Nilsson (2018) *Children in Minority Religions: Growing Up in Controversial Religious Groups*. Sheffield: Equinox.

Gallagher, Eugene V. (ed.) (2017) *'Cult Wars' in Historical Perspective: New and Minority Religions*. London: Routledge.

Gallagher, Sally K. (2003) *Evangelical Identity and Gendered Family Life*. New Brunswick, NJ: Rutgers University Press.

Giambalvo, Carol, Michael Kropveld and Michael Langone (2013) 'Changes in North American Cult Awareness Organizations' in Eileen Barker (ed.) *Revision and Diversification in New Religious Movements*. London: Routledge, pp. 227–47.

Goldman, Marion S. (1999) *Passionate Journeys: Why Successful Women Joined a Cult*. Ann Arbor: The University of Michigan Press.

Goodwin, Megan (2020) *Abusing Religion: Literary Persecution, Sex Scandals, and American Minority Religions*. New Brunswick, NJ: Rutgers University Press.

Graham-Hyde, Edward (2023) 'From Bad to Worse: The Evolving Nature of "Cult" Rhetoric in the Wake of COVID-19 and QAnon'. *Implicit Religion: Journal for the Critical Study of Religion* 24(2): 135–59.

Grendele, Windy A., Maya Flax and Savin Bapir-Tardy (2023) 'Shunning from the Jehovah's Witness Community: Is It Legal'? *Journal of Law and Religion* 38(2): 290–313.

Griffith, Marie R. (1997) *God's Daughters: Evangelical Women and the Power of Submission*. California: University of California Press.

Gutgsell, J. (2017) 'A Loving Provision'? How Former Jehovah's Witnesses Experience Shunning Practices. Unpublished Master's Thesis. Brussels: Vrije Universiteit Brussel.

Hall, David D. (ed.) (1997) *Lived Religion in America: Toward a History of Practice*. Princeton, NJ: Princeton University Press.

Hardyment, Christina (1983) *Dream Babies: Child Care from Locke to Spock*. London: Jonathan Cape.

Harvey, Sarah and Suzanne Newcombe (2021) 'Gender and Contemporary Millennial Movements' in James Crossley and Alastair Lockhart (eds.) *Critical Dictionary of Apocalyptic and Millenarian Movements*. www.cdamm.org/articles/gender-and-contemporary (accessed 14 February 2025).

Hassan, Steven (1988) *Combatting Cult Mind Control*. Rochester, VT: Park Street Press.

Heelas, Paul and Linda Woodhead, with Benjamin Steel, Bronislaw Szersynski and Karin Tusting (2005) *The Spiritual Revolution: Why Religion Is Giving Way to Spirituality*. Oxford: Blackwell.

Helmore, Edward (2019) 'Nxivm Trial: Keith Raniere Found Guilty on All Counts in Sex Cult Case'. *The Guardian*, 19 June. www.theguardian.com/us-news/2019/jun/19/nxivm-trial-keith-raniere-verdict-guilty-allison-mack (accessed 14 February 2025).

Hofmann, David C. and Lorne L. Dawson (2014) 'The Neglected Role of Charismatic Authority in the Study of Terrorist Groups and Radicalization'. *Studies in Conflict & Terrorism* 37: 348–68.

Home Office (April 2022) *Controlling or Coercive Behaviour Statutory Guidance Framework*. https://assets.publishing.service.gov.uk/media/626cffcbd3bf7f0e7947f3a4/MASTER_ENGLISH_-Draft_Controlling_or_Coercive_Behaviour_Statutory_Guidance.pdf (accessed 14 February 2025).

Hong, Nansook (1998) *In the Shadow of the Moons: My Life in the Reverend Sun Myung Moon's Family*. Boston, MA: Little, Brown.

Hunt, Stephen J. (2003) *Alternative Religions: A Sociological Approach*. Aldershot: Ashgate.

Independent Inquiry Child Sexual Abuse (2021) *Child Protection in Religious Organisations and Settings: Investigation Report*. House of Commons. https://webarchive.nationalarchives.gov.uk/ukgwa/20221216171718/https://www.iicsa.org.uk/key-documents/26895/view/child-protection-religious-organisa

tions-settings-investigation-report-september-2021-.pdf (accessed 14 February 2025).

Inge, Annabel (2016) *The Making of a Salafi Woman: Paths to Conversion*. Oxford: Oxford University Press.

Ingersoll, Julie (2003) *Evangelical Christian Women: War Stories in the Gender Battles*. New York: New York University Press.

International Cultic Studies Association (2013) 'Dialogue and Cultic Studies: Why Dialogue Benefits the Cultic Studies Field'. *ICSA Today* 4(3): 2–7. www.icsahome.com/home/aboutus/benefitsofdialogue (accessed 14 February 2025).

Introvigne, Massimo (2021a) 'The England-Wales Independent Inquiry into Child Sexual Abuse: Jehovah's Witnesses and the So-called Two-Witness Rule'. *Bitter Winter*. https://bitterwinter.org/the-england-wales-independent-inquiry-into-child-sexual-abuse-jehovahs-witnesses-and-the-so-called-two-witness-rule/ (accessed 17 April 2025).

Introvigne, Massimo (2021b) 'Jehovah's Witnesses Win Important Case in Belgium'. *Bitter Winter*. https://bitterwinter.org/jehovahs-witnesses-win-important-case-in-belgium/ (accessed 14 February 2025).

Introvigne, Massimo (2022a) *Brainwashing: Reality or Myth?* Cambridge: Cambridge University Press.

Introvigne, Massimo (2022b) 'Ghent Decision Overturned on Appeal: Jehovah's Witnesses' Shunning Can Be Freely Taught and Practiced in Belgium'. *Bitter Winter*. https://bitterwinter.org/ghent-decision-overturned-jehovahs-witnesses/ (accessed 14 February 2025).

Introvigne, Massimo (2023) 'Norway: Why the European Court of Human Rights Rejected a Complaint from a Disfellowshipped Former Jehovah's Witness'. *Bitter Winter*. https://bitterwinter.org/european-court-rejected-a-complaint-from-a-disfellowshipped-jehovahs-witness/ (accessed 14 February 2025).

Introvigne, Massimo and James T. Richardson (2022) 'The Family Survival Trust 2022 Report on "Cults": Reviving the Dead Horse of "Brainwashing"'. *Bitter Winter*. https://bitterwinter.org/the-family-survival-trust-2022-reports-on-cults/ (accessed 14 February 2025).

Jacobs, Janet (1989) *Divine Disenchantment: Deconverting from New Religions*. Bloomington: Indiana University Press.

Jacobs, Janet (1991) 'Gender and Power in New Religious Movements: A Feminist Discourse on the Scientific Study of Religion'. *Religion* 21(4): 345–56.

Jacobs, Janet (2007) 'Abuse in New Religious Movements: Challenges for the Sociology of Religion' in David G. Bromley (ed.) *Teaching New Religious Movements*. Oxford: Oxford University Press, pp. 231–44.

Jenkins, Kathleen E. (2005) *Awesome Families: The Promise of Healing Relationships in the International Churches of Christ*. New Brunswick, NJ: Rutgers University Press.

Jesus Fellowship Church (1991) *New Creation Community Church Precepts*. Northampton: Jesus Fellowship Church.

Jesus Fellowship Church (2000) *We Believe: An Introduction to the Faith and Practice of the Jesus Fellowship*. Northampton: Multiply Productions.

Jesus Fellowship Church (2007) *Jesus: The Name, The Foundation*. Northampton: Jesus Fellowship Church.

Jesus Fellowship Community Trust (2021) *Closure Statement*. https://jesus.org.uk/wp-content/uploads/2022/06/Redress-Scheme-Closure-Statement-Final-UPDATED.pdf (accessed 14 February 2025).

Jesus Fellowship Community Trust (2024) *Final Report: Jesus Fellowship Redress Scheme*. https://jesus.org.uk/wp-content/uploads/2024/09/Jesus-Fellowship-Redress-Scheme-Final-Report-Print-Version.pdf (accessed 14 February 2025).

Jesus Fellowship Survivors Association (2018) *Information Sheet for Counsellors*.

Jesus Fellowship Survivors Association (2020) *Redress Scheme Wish List Produced by the JFSA*. https://jesusfellowshipsurvivors.org/redress-scheme-wish-list-produced-by-the-jfsa/ (accessed 14 February 2025).

Jones, Kristina, Celeste Jones and Juliana Buhring (2008) *Not Without My Sister: The True Story of Three Girls Violated and Betrayed*. New York: Harper Element.

Joosse, Paul and Robin Willey (2020) 'Gender and Charismatic Power'. *Theory and Society* 49(4): 533–61.

Kay, William K. (2004) 'The Jesus Fellowship (Jesus Army)' in Christopher Partridge (ed.) *Encyclopedia of New Religions: A Guide*. Oxford: Lion, pp. 89–90.

Kay, William K. (2007) *Apostolic Networks in Britain: New Ways of Being Church*. Eugene, OR: Wipf & Stock.

Keenan, Marie (2012) *Child Sexual Abuse and the Catholic Church: Gender, Power and Organizational Culture*. Oxford: Oxford University Press.

Kent, Stephen (1997) 'Brainwashing In Scientology's Rehabilitation Project Force (RPF)'. Revised Version of a Presentation at the Society for the Scientific Study of Religion, San Diego, California, 7 November. https://skent.ualberta.ca/contributions/scientology/brainwashing-in-scientologys-rehabilitation-project-force-rpf/ (accessed 14 February 2025).

Langone, Michael D. (ed.) (1994) *Recovery from Cults: Help for Victims of Psychological and Spiritual Abuse*. New York: W. W. Norton.

Langone, Michael D. (2015) 'Characteristics Associated with Cultic Groups'. *ICSA Today* 6(3). https://articles1.icsahome.com/articles/characteristics (accessed 14 February 2025).

Laycock, Joseph (2022) *New Religious Movements: The Basics*. London: Routledge.

Laycock, Joseph P. (2024) 'A Cult by Any Other Name: Is "High Demand Group" a Useful Category?'. *Nova Religio* 28(1): 90–104.

Lee, Ellie, Jennie Bristow, Charlotte Faircloth and Jan Macvarish (2014) *Parenting Culture Studies*. Basingstoke: Palgrave Macmillan.

Lewis, James R. (ed.) (2011) *Violence and New Religious Movements*. Oxford: Oxford University Press.

Lewis, James R. (2014) 'Violence' in George D. Chryssides and Benjamin E. Zeller (eds.) *The Bloomsbury Companion to New Religious Movements*. London: Bloomsbury, pp. 149–62.

Lewis, James R. and J. Gordon Melton (eds.) (1994) *Sex, Slander and Salvation: Investigating the Family/Children of God*. Stanford, CA: Center for Academic Publications.

Lifton, Robert J. (1961) *Thought Reform and the Psychology of Totalism: A Study of 'Brainwashing' in China*. New York: Norton.

Lloyd, Vincent W. (2018) *In Defense of Charisma*. New York: Columbia University Press.

Lucia, Amanda (2018) 'Guru Sex: Charisma, Proxemic Desire, and the Haptic Logics of the Guru-Disciple Relationship'. *Journal of the American Academy of Religion* 86(4): 953–88.

Lukes, Steven (2004) *Power: A Radical View*. London: Red Globe Press.

Lynch, Gordon (2012) 'Living with Two Cultural Turns: The Case of the Study of Religion' in Sasha Roseneil and Stephen Frosh (eds.) *Social Research after the Cultural Turn*. Basingstoke: Palgrave Macmillan, pp. 73–92.

Lynch, Gordon (2015) *Remembering Child Migration: Faith, Nation-Building and the Wounds of Charity*. London: Bloomsbury.

Lynch, Gordon (2022) '"To See a Sinner Repent Is a Joyful Thing": Moral Cultures and the Sexual Abuse of Children in the Christian Church' in David Henig, Anna Strhan and Joel Robbins (eds.) *Where Is the Good in the World?: Ethical Life between Social Theory and Philosophy*. New York: Berghahn Books, pp. 123–41.

Maaga, Mary McCormick (1998) *Hearing the Voices of Jonestown*. New York: Syracuse University Press.

Maddox, Marion (2013) '"Rise Up Warrior Princess Daughters": Is Evangelical Women's Submission a Mere Fairy Tale'? *Journal of Feminist Studies in Religion* 29(1): 9–26.

McClenaghan, Maeve (2022) '"Exposed to Horrendous Things": Young People in UK Speak Out against Evangelical Church'. *The Guardian*, 29 November. www.theguardian.com/world/2022/nov/29/young-uk-people-speak-out-against-evangelical-church-universal-kingdom-god (accessed 14 February 2025).

McCutcheon, Russell (1997) *Manufacturing Religion: The Discourse of Sui Generis Religion and the Politics of Nostalgia*. Oxford: Oxford University Press.

McGuire, Meredith B. (2003) 'Gendered Spiritualities' in James A. Beckford and James T. Richardson (eds.) *Challenging Religion: Essays in Honour of Eileen Barker*. London: Routledge, pp. 170–80.

McGuire, Meredith B. (2008) *Lived Religion: Faith and Practice in Everyday Life*. Oxford: Oxford University Press.

McPhillips, Kathleen and Sarah-Jane Page (2021) 'Introduction: Religion, Gender and Violence'. *Religion and Gender* 11(2): 151–65.

Mellor, Philip A. and Chris Shilling (2010) 'Body Pedagogics and the Religious Habitus: A New Direction for the Sociological Study of Religion'. *Religion* 40(1): 27–38.

Melton, John Gordon (1994) 'Sexuality and the Maturation of the Family' in James R. Lewis and J. Gordon Melton (eds.) *Sex, Slander and Salvation: Investigating the Family/Children of God*. Stanford, CA: Center for Academic Publications, pp. 71–97.

Melton, John Gordon (2004) 'Perspective: Toward a Definition of "New Religion".' *Nova Religio* 8(1): 73–87.

Miller, Timothy (2013) *Spiritual and Visionary Communities: Out to Save the World*. London: Routledge.

Montell, Amanda (2021) *Cultish: The Language of Fanaticism*. New York: HarperWave.

Moore, Rebecca (2009) *Understanding Jonestown and Peoples Temple*. London: Bloomsbury.

Moore, Rebecca (2012) 'Peoples Temple'. *World Religions and Spirituality Project*. www.wrldrels.org/profiles/PeoplesTemple.htm (accessed 14 February 2025).

Moore, Rebecca (2018) *Beyond Brainwashing: Perspectives on Cultic Violence*. Cambridge: Cambridge University Press.

Moore, Rebecca (2021) 'Apocalyptic Groups and Charisma of the Cadre' in José Pedro Zúquete (ed.) *Routledge International Handbook of Charisma*. London: Routledge, pp. 277–87.

Moslener, Sara (2015) *Virgin Nation: Sexual Purity and American Adolescence*. Oxford: Oxford University Press.

Nason-Clark, Nancy (2000) 'Making the Sacred Safe: Woman Abuse and Communities of Faith'. *Sociology of Religion* 61(4): 349–68.

Nason-Clark, Nancy (2003) 'The Making of a Survivor: Rhetoric and Reality in the Study of Religion and Abuse' in James A. Beckford and James T. Richardson (eds.) *Challenging Religion: Essays in Honour of Eileen Barker*. London: Routledge, pp. 181–92.

Neitz, Mary Jo and Marion S. Goldman (eds.) (1995) *Sex, Lies, and Sanctity: Religion and Deviance in Contemporary North America*. Religion and the Social Order, Vol. 5. Leeds: Emerald Group.

Nevalainen, Kirsti L. (2011) *Change of Blood Lineage through Ritual Sex in the Unification Church*. Breinigsville, PA: BookSurge.

Newcombe, Suzanne and Sarah Harvey (2024) 'Balancing Pragmatism and Precision: Inform's Approach to Cult Rhetoric' in Aled Thomas and Edward Graham-Hyde (eds.) *'Cult' Rhetoric in the 21st Century: Deconstructing the Study of New Religious Movements*. London: Bloomsbury, pp. 35–62.

Newland, Tahlia (2019) 'Does Tibetan Buddhism Condone Abuse'? *Beyond The Temple* website, 17 March. https://beyondthetemple.com/does-tibetan-buddhism-condone-abuse/ (accessed 14 February 2025).

Niebuhr, Helmut Richard (1929) *The Social Sources of Denominationalism*. Whitefish, MT: Kessinger (2004 edition).

Nilsson, Sanja (2024) *Children in New Religious Movements*. Cambridge: Cambridge University Press.

Nye, Malory (2019) 'Decolonizing the Study of Religion'. *Open Library of Humanities* 5(1): 43.

Oakley, Lisa (2018) 'Understanding Spiritual Abuse'. *Church Times*, 16 February. www.churchtimes.co.uk/articles/2018/16-february/comment/opinion/understanding-spiritual-abuse (accessed 14 February 2025).

Oakley, Lisa and Justin Humphreys (2019) *Escaping the Maze of Spiritual Abuse: Creating Healthy Christian Cultures*. London: SPCK.

Oakley, Lisa and Kathryn Kinmond (2016) 'The Relationship between Spiritual Abuse and Domestic Violence and Abuse in Faith Based Communities' in Sarah Hilder and Vanessa Bettinson (eds.) *Domestic Violence: Interdisciplinary Perspectives on Protection, Prevention and Intervention*. Basingstoke: Palgrave Macmillan, pp. 203–26.

Orsi, Robert A. (2004) *Between Heaven and Earth: The Religious Worlds People Make and the Scholars Who Study Them*. Princeton, NJ: Princeton University Press.

Orsi, Robert A. (2019) 'The Study of Religion on the Other Side of Disgust: Modern Catholic Sexuality Is a Dark and Troubled Landscape'. *Harvard*

*Divinity Bulletin.* https://bulletin.hds.harvard.edu/the-study-of-religion-on-the-other-side-of-disgust/ (accessed 14 February 2025).

Palmer, Susan (1994) *Moon Sisters, Krishna Mothers, Rajneesh Lovers: Women's Roles in New Religions.* Syracuse, NY: University of Syracuse Press.

Palmer, Susan (2016) Children in Sectarian Religions and State Control, 1950–2020. SSHRC Insight Grant. www.spiritualchildhoods.ca/ (accessed 14 February 2025).

Palmer, Susan and Charlotte Hardman (eds.) (1999) *Children in New Religions.* New Brunswick, NJ: Rutgers University Press.

Pattison, Stephen (2000) *Shame: Theory, Therapy, Theology.* Cambridge: Cambridge University Press.

Peluso, Daniela, Emily Sinclair, Beatriz Labate and Clancy Cavnar (2020) 'Reflections on Crafting an Ayahuasca Community Guide for the Awareness of Sexual Abuse'. *Journal of Psychedelic Studies* 4(1): 24–33.

Pentikäinen, Juha, Jurgen F. K. Redhardt and Michael York (2002) 'The Church of Scientology's Rehabilitation Project Force'. *CESNUR.* www.cesnur.org/2002/scient_rpf_02.htm (accessed 14 February 2025).

Ploeg, Luke Vander (2017) 'Lack of Education Leads to Lost Dreams and Low Income for Many Jehovah's Witnesses'. *NPR,* 19 February. www.npr.org/2017/02/19/510585965/poor-education-leads-to-lost-dreams-and-low-income-for-many-jehovahs-witnesses (accessed 14 February 2025).

Pratezina, Jessica (2019) 'Alternative Religion Kids: Spiritual and Cultural Identity among Children and Youth Involved with New Religious Movements'. *International Journal of Children's Spirituality* 24(1): 73–82.

Prophet, Erin (2016) 'Charisma and Authority in New Religious Movements' in James Lewis and Inga Bårdsen Tøllefsen (eds.) *Oxford Handbook of New Religious Movements* vol. 2. Oxford: Oxford University Press, pp. 36–49.

Prophet, Erin. (2017). 'Elizabeth Clare Prophet: Gender, Sexuality and the Divine Feminine' in Inga Bårdsen Tøllefsen and Christian Giudice (eds.) *Female Leaders of New Religious Movements.* London: Palgrave Macmillan, pp. 51–77.

Prophet, Erin (2018) *Coercion or Conversion? A Case Study in Religion and the Law: CUT v. Mull v. Prophet 1986.* Gainesville, FL: Linden Books.

Puttick, Elizabeth (1997) *Women in New Religions: In Search of Community, Sexuality and Spiritual Power.* Basingstoke: Palgrave Macmillan.

Ransom, Heather (2022) 'Leaving the Jehovah's Witnesses; Identity, Transition and Recovery'. Unpublished PhD thesis. Edge Hill University.

Ransom, Heather, Rebecca L. Monk and Derek Heim (2021) 'Grieving the Living: The Social Death of Former Jehovah's Witnesses'. *Journal of Religion and Health* 61: 2458–80.

Reichert, Jenny, James T. Richardson and Rebecca Thomas (2015) '"Brainwashing": Diffusion of a Questionable Concept in Legal Systems'. *International Journal for the Study of New Religions* 6(1), 3–26.

Richardson, James T. (2021) 'The Myth of the Omnipotent Leader: The Social Construction of a Misleading Account of Leadership in New Religious Movements'. *Nova Religio* 24: 11–25.

Rochford, E. Burke Jr. and Jennifer Heinlein (1998) 'Child Abuse in the Hare Krishna Movement: 1971–1986'. *ISKCON Communications Journal* 6(1): 43–69.

Rosedale, Herbert and Langone, Michael D. (2015) 'On Using the Term "Cult"'. *ICSA Today* 6(3): 4–6. www.icsahome.com/elibrary/topics/articles/onusingtermcult (accessed 14 February 2025).

Royal Commission into Institutional Responses to Child Sexual Abuse (2016) *Case Study 29: Jehovah's Witnesses*. www.childabuseroyalcommission.gov.au/case-studies/case-study-29-jehovahs-witnesses (accessed 14 February 2025).

Rutter, Peter (1989) *Sex in the Forbidden Zone: When Therapists, Doctors, Clergy, Teachers and Other Men in Power Betray Women's Trust*. New York: Fawcett.

Scorer, Richard (2014) *Betrayed: The English Catholic Church and the Sex Abuse Crisis*. London: Biteback.

Sessions, Erin and Bernard Doherty (2023) '"Cults", Coercion, and Control: Rhetoric, Reality, and the Return of "Brainwashing"?' *Implicit Religion: Journal for the Critical Study of Religion* 24(2): 161–94.

Shorter, Rosie C. (2021) 'Rethinking Complementarianism: Sydney Anglicans, Orthodoxy and Gendered Inequality'. *Religion and Gender* 11(2): 218–44.

Shupe, Anson D. (1995) *In the Name of All That's Holy: A Theory of Clergy Malfeasance*. Westport, CT: Praeger.

Shupe, Anson D. (2007) *Spoils of the Kingdom: Clergy Misconduct and Religious Community*. Champagne: University of Illinois Press.

Shupe, Anson D., William A. Stacey and Susan E. Darnell (2000) *Bad Pastors: Clergy Misconduct in Modern America*. New York: New York University Press.

Singler, Beth and Eileen Barker (eds.) (2022) *Radical Transformations in Minority Religions*. London: Routledge.

Sointu, Eeva and Linda Woodhead (2008) 'Spirituality, Gender, and Expressive Selfhood'. *Journal for the Scientific Study of Religion* 47(2): 259–76.

Stark, Evan (2007) *Coercive Control: How Men Entrap Women in Personal Life*. Oxford: Oxford University Press.

Stausberg, Michael, Alexander Van Der Haven and Erica Baffelli (2023) 'Religious Minorities: Conceptual Perspectives'. *Religious Minorities Online*. www.degruyter.com/database/RMO/entry/rmo.23389320/html?lang=en (accessed 14 February 2025).

Strhan, Anna (2019) *The Figure of the Child in Contemporary Evangelicalism*. Oxford: Oxford University Press.

Sweet, Paige (2019) 'The Sociology of Gaslighting'. *American Sociological Review* 84(5): 851–75.

Thomas, Aled and Edward Graham-Hyde (2023) 'Introduction: The Return of the "Cult"'. *Implicit Religion: Journal for the Critical Study of Religion* 24(2): 129–34.

Thomas, Aled and Edward Graham-Hyde (eds.) (2024) *'Cult' Rhetoric in the 21st Century: Deconstructing the Study of New Religious Movements*. London: Bloomsbury.

Thwaites, Chrissie (2022) 'The Impact of Christian Purity Culture Is Still Being Felt – Including in Britain'. *The Conversation*, 28 June. https://theconversation.com/the-impact-of-christian-purity-culture-is-still-being-felt-including-in-britain-182907 (accessed 14 February 2025).

Troeltsch, Ernst (1931) *The Social Teachings of the Christian Churches*. New York: Harper and Row.

Urban, Hugh B. (2003) *Tantra: Sex, Secrecy, Politics, and Power in the Study of Religion*. Berkeley: University of California Press.

van Eck Duymaer van Twist, Amanda (ed.) (2014) *Minority Religions and Fraud: In Good Faith*. Farnham: Ashgate.

van Eck Duymaer van Twist, Amanda (2015) *Perfect Children: Growing Up on the Religious Fringe*. Oxford: Oxford University Press.

Vance, Laura (2015) *Women in New Religions*. New York: New York University Press.

Wallis, Roy (1984) *The Elementary Forms of the New Religious Life*. London: Routledge.

Watchtower Online Library (2024) *The Watchtower Announcing Jehovah's Kingdom – Study Edition August*. https://wol.jw.org/en/wol/library/r1/lp-e/all-publications/watchtower/the-watchtower-2024/study-edition/august (accessed 14 February 2025).

Weber, Max (1922) *The Theory of Social and Economic Organization*. New York: Free Press.

Weber, Max (1968) *Economy and Society: An Outline of Interpretive Sociology*. New York: Bedminster Press.

Welter, Barbara (1966) 'The Cult of True Womanhood: 1820–1860'. *American Quarterly* 18(2) Part 1 (Summer): 151–74.

Wessinger, Catherine (1993) *Women's Leadership in Marginal Religions: Explorations Outside the Mainstream*. Champaign: University of Illinois Press.

Wessinger, Catherine (2000) *How the Millennium Comes Violently: From Jonestown to Heaven's Gate*. New York: Seven Bridges Press.

Wessinger, Catherine (2008) 'The Problem Is Totalism, Not "Cults": Reflections on the Thirtieth Anniversary of Jonestown'. *The Jonestown Report* Vol. 10. https://jonestown.sdsu.edu/?page_id=31459 (accessed 14 February 2025).

White, Nadine and Emma Youle (2019) 'SPAC Nation: What We Know about Church Whose Members Are Accused of Fraud and Abuse'. *Huffington Post*, 16 December. www.huffingtonpost.co.uk/entry/spac-nation-fraud-abuse-panorama_uk_5df6e471e4b03aed50f0650b (accessed 14 February 2025).

Wilcox, Melissa M. (2011) 'Gender Roles, Sexuality and Children in Millennial Movements' in Catherine Wessinger (ed.) *The Oxford Handbook of Millennialism*. Oxford: Oxford University Press, pp. 171–90.

Wilkins, Leslie (1967) *Social Deviance*. London: Routledge.

Wilson, Bryan (1961) *Sects and Society: A Sociological Study of the Elim Tabernacle, Christan Science, and Christadelphians*. Berkeley: University of California Press.

Wilson, Bryan (1990) *The Social Dimensions of Sectarianism: Sects and New Religious Movements in Contemporary Society*. Oxford: Clarendon Press.

Wright, Stuart A. and Susan J. Palmer (2015) 'The Twelve Tribes' in Stuart A. Wright and Susan J. Palmer (eds.) *Storming Zion: Government Raids on Religious Communities*. New York: Oxford University Press, pp. 47–72.

Yinger, Milton (1946) *Religion in the Struggle for Power*. Durham, NC: Duke University Press.

Zablocki, Benjamin and Thomas Robbins (eds.) (2001) *Misunderstanding Cults: Searching for Objectivity in a Controversial Field*. Toronto: University of Toronto Press.

Zeller, Benjamin E. (2023) 'Cult' in George D. Chryssides and Amy R. Whitehead (eds.) *Contested Concepts in the Study of Religion: A Critical Exploration*. London: Bloomsbury, pp.27–33.

# Acknowledgements

Funding from the Arts and Humanities Research Council (AHRC), grant number AH/W003112/1, made it possible for this Element to be published Open Access, making the digital version freely available for anyone to read and reuse under a Creative Commons licence.

Thank you to Rebecca Moore, editor of this Elements series, both for accepting my manuscript and for your supportive and constructive comments on it throughout the submission and revision process. Thanks also to Ann Gleig and James T. Richardson, whose helpful suggestions have made this a stronger piece of work.

Thank you to the 'Abuse in Religious Contexts' team: Gordon Lynch, Linda Woodhead, Johanna Stiebert, Lisa Oakley, Justin Humphreys, Richard Scorer, Eve Parker, Jo Kind, Yehudis Fletcher, Yasmin Rehman and Jenny Hardy. Our regular meetings and discussions over the course of this project have shaped this Element and I have learnt a great deal from every one of you. Special thanks to Gordon Lynch, the Principal Investigator, not only for initiating the project but for steering us through it so thoughtfully, and to Gordon Lynch and Johanna Stiebert for reading drafts of this Element and for your insightful comments and your careful copy editing.

I am indebted, as always, to my Inform colleagues, past and present, who influence my thinking in so many important ways. Thanks in particular to those who have read and commented upon the sections of this Element: Eileen Barker, George Chryssides, Suzanne Newcombe and Amanda van Eck Duymaer van Twist. Your pioneering work is reflected in this Element, although any errors are my own. Thank you to all the former members, victims and survivors who have shared their stories with Inform over the years. I hope this Element does justice to your experiences.

# Cambridge Elements

## New Religious Movements

### Founding Editor
†James R. Lewis
*Wuhan University*

The late James R. Lewis was a Professor of Philosophy at Wuhan University, China. He was the author or co-author of 128 articles and reference book entries, and editor or co-editor of 50 books. He was also the general editor for the *Alternative Spirituality and Religion Review* and served as the associate editor for the *Journal of Religion and Violence*. His prolific publications include *The Cambridge Companion to Religion and Terrorism* (Cambridge University Press 2017) and *Falun Gong: Spiritual Warfare and Martyrdom* (Cambridge University Press 2018).

### Series Editor
Rebecca Moore
*San Diego State University*

Rebecca Moore is Emerita Professor of Religious Studies at San Diego State University. She has written and edited numerous books and articles on Peoples Temple and the Jonestown tragedy. Publications include *Beyond Brainwashing: Perspectives on Cultic Violence* (Cambridge University Press 2018) and *Peoples Temple and Jonestown in the Twenty-First Century* (Cambridge University Press 2022). She is reviews editor for *Nova Religio*, the quarterly journal on new and emergent religions published by the University of Pennsylvania Press.

### About the Series

Elements in New Religious Movements go beyond cult stereotypes and popular prejudices to present new religions and their adherents in a scholarly and engaging manner. Case studies of individual groups, such as Transcendental Meditation and Scientology, provide in-depth consideration of some of the most well known, and controversial, groups. Thematic examinations of women, children, science, technology, and other topics focus on specific issues unique to these groups. Historical analyses locate new religions in specific religious, social, political, and cultural contexts. These examinations demonstrate why some groups exist in tension with the wider society and why others live peaceably in the mainstream. The series highlights the differences, as well as the similarities, within this great variety of religious expressions.

# Cambridge Elements

# New Religious Movements

## Elements in the Series

*Managing Religion and Religious Changes in Iran: A Socio-Legal Analysis*
Sajjad Adeliyan Tous and James T. Richardson

*Children in New Religious Movements*
Sanja Nilsson

*The Sacred Force of Star Wars Jedi*
William Sims Bainbridge

*Mormonism*
Matthew Bowman

*Jehovah's Witnesses*
Jolene Chu and Ollimatti Peltonen

*Wearing Their Faith: New Religious Movements, Dress, and Fashion in America*
Lynn S. Neal

*Santa Muerte Devotion: Vulnerability, Protection, Intimacy*
Wil G. Pansters

*J. Krishnamurti: Self-Inquiry, Awakening, and Transformation*
Constance A. Jones

*Making Places Sacred: New Articulations of Place and Power*
Matt Tomlinson and Yujie Zhu

*Korean New Religions*
Don Baker

*The Revelation Spiritual Home: The Revival of African Indigenous Spirituality*
Massimo Introvigne and Rosita Šorytė

*Abuse in New Religious Movements*
Sarah Harvey

A full series listing is available at: www.cambridge.org/ENRM